HOW TO IDENTIFY MUSHROOMS TO GENUS I

HOW TO IDENTIFY
MUSHROOMS
TO GENUS I:
Macroscopic Features

BY DAVID L. LARGENT

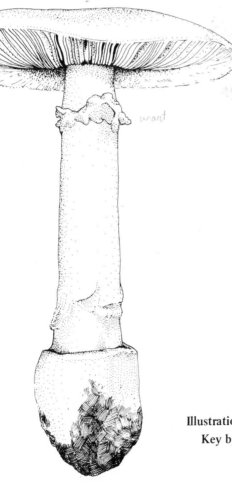

pileus

wart

Illustrations by Sharon Hadley
Key by Daniel E. Stuntz

David L. Largent
Biology Department
Humboldt State University
Arcata, California 95521

Sharon Hadley
P.O. Box 121
Paisley, Oregon
97636

Daniel E. Stuntz
Botany Department
University of Washington
Seattle, Washington 98195

MAD RIVER PRESS INC.

Published by Mad River Press, Inc.
Route 2, Box 151B
Eureka, CA 95501

Printed by Eureka Printing Co., Inc.
106 T Street
Eureka, CA 95501

ISBN 0-916-422-00-3

To my wife, Pamela.

TABLE OF CONTENTS

LIST OF PLATES

LIST OF FIGURES

PREFACE TO THE FIRST EDITION

For the past five years I have been teaching a course on fleshy fungi through the Extension School of California State University, Humboldt. The most common question asked of me by students, amateur mycologists, or casual observers is,

"How do you tell poisonous from edible mushrooms?"

The only way to tell edible from non-edible mushrooms is to know what the name of the mushroom is, then look up this in a reference book to see if it has been safely eaten before.

There are a number of good reference books on mushrooms. Some of them are . . .

Lange & Hora	*A Guide to Mushrooms and Toadstools*
O. K. Miller	*Mushrooms of North America*
Smith	*The Mushroom Hunter's Field Guide*
Stuntz	*The Savory Wild Mushroom*

All of these contain pictures and short descriptions of the most commonly encountered fleshy fungi.

But an important omission in all of these reference books is a complete, well-illustrated portion explaining the fundamental features that a professional mycologist uses to name (identify) fleshy fungi. The best available source of information on features used to identify fungi is Alexander H. Smith's *Mushrooms in their Natural Habitats*. It contains chapters on macroscopic and microscopic characteristics but is difficult to use.

The purpose of this book is to teach the reader how to identify mushrooms **using only macroscopic features** of the fruiting body. Macroscopic features, or those that can be seen with the naked eye, require no special equipment and are thus useful for everyone. Included at the end of this manual is a key to many of the mushroom genera using only the macroscopic characters herein described. A second volume is planned to follow that will deal with microscopic features.

This book began as a mimeographed, non-illustrated list of features used in mushroom identification put together by Harriet Peters (now Harriet Burge) and myself in 1961. At that time we were both studying under Dr. H. D. Thiers of San Francisco State College. The mimeographed lists have since been revised and enlarged by Dr. Thiers and myself in our respective courses in the study of fungi. I would like to here acknowledge and express my gratitude to Dr. Thiers for introducing me to the world of fungi and for his patience and encouragement in teaching me so much about this area that has become my major professional interest.

The concept of *habit type* (grouping mushrooms with similar features) is used by Dr. Daniel E. Stuntz in his tutorage of thousands of amateur mushroom hunters throughout the Pacific Northwest. I was fortunate enough to also have studied under Dr. Stuntz, and am very grateful to him for fostering my interest and for continuing to direct my education in the fungi. I am further indebted to the Puget Sound Mycological Society, whose scientific advisor is Dr. Stuntz, since the idea for the section of this book on "How to Collect Mushrooms" (p 49-50) resulted from their summary of a similar article in one of their news letters.

I want to especially acknowledge my partner in this crime, Sharon Hadley, who did the drawings for this book. I have never met a more bright and cheerful person, nor a more broadly knowledgeable amateur naturalist.

Finally, I wish to dedicate this book to my wife Pamela. I thank her for her constant companionship at home and in the field, for her help in typing, and for just being herself. She made this book possible.

David L. Largent
Eureka, California
October, 1973

PREFACE TO THE SECOND EDITION

This book has now been used by various agaricologists, amateurs and professionals alike, for three and one half years. It has been reprinted five times and has received numerous positive comments; therefore it appears to have achieved its purpose. I am extremely grateful for that and would like to take this space to thank everyone who has found this book useful.

I would like to acknowledge more specifically the contributions of Dr. Daniel E. Stuntz. Not only did I copy the concept of *habit type* from him but I also used his keys. These parts of this book should be attributed more to his knowledge and efforts than to mine. Furthermore I would like to take this opportunity to say that I consider him to be one of the most outstanding human beings I have ever met. Stand proud Daniel E. Stuntz, you have every right to do so.

The information contained within this edition is basically the same as the first edition except for grammatical errors and a few technical changes (such as the use of Naucorioid and Annellarioid, for example) which were gratefully made by Roy Watling. Not only did he make them once, but twice; it seems I mislaid the first changes. So, Roy, please accept my thanks as well as my apologies.

I failed to give Charlie Brown his due in the first edition of this book. Several of the drawings were his: Plate 12, Fig. A; Plate 15, Figs. A, B; Plate 16, Fig. C as well as Figures 8 and 9. All the other drawings were done by Sharon Hadley who has received "super-kudos" from everyone. If anyone wants to contact Sharon, she can be reached at the following address: P. O. Box 121, Paisley Oregon. 97636. Write her; she will be delighted.

Finally I wish to rededicate this book to my wife, Pamela. My life has become delightfully calm since I married her in 1970. Everyone should be lucky enough to find their Pamela. Thanks Pam, I love you.

David L. Largent
Eureka, California
July, 1977

INTRODUCTION

A mushroom is the "fruiting body" often called a basidiocarp of a fungus. The fruiting body is the structure that bears the microscopic propagules called **spores** that reproduce the fungus. A mushroom is therefore similar to an apple on a tree — the apple bears small seeds which ultimately reproduce the tree.

The remainder of the fungus is called the **vegetative** (feeding) portion, and consists of microscopic filaments called **hyphae** (singular **hypha**) which form a mass known as the **mycelium**. Fungal mycelia occur in a wide variety of substrates. If the mycelium grows in the soil, the substrate is said to be **terrestrial**; if it grows in wood, it is called **lignicolous**; if in dung, it is called **coprophilous**; occasionally, mushroom mycelia grow in other mushrooms, and this is known as a **fungicolous** substrate.

The mycelium obtains food from the organic products present in these various substrates by liberating enzymes that break down complex compounds, such as cellulose and lignin, into soluble products. The soluble products are then absorbed and used by the hyphae as food, resulting in growth of the mycelium.

The mycelium continues to grow as long as the combination of various environmental factors (such as moisture, temperature, pH, C/N ratio) remains favorable. The proper combination of factors varies with every fungus. It appears that biological factors are often important. For example, many fungi are found only associated with certain kinds of trees. (In some of these cases, the mycelium is known to form a symbiotic relationship with the tree roots called a **mycorrhizal association**.)

At some point in the development of the mycelium, presumably due to subtle alterations in the various physical, chemical and biological factors that comprise the fungal environment, changes occur that eventually result in the formation of the reproductive stage, the mushroom. The factors causing the shift from vegetative to reproductive growth are not understood, but moisture seems to be important. But even though the cause of the changes is unknown, the changes themselves are well-documented.

Two kinds of mycelia are necessary for the changes to begin. They differ in the nature of their nuclei. The mycelia look alike, but belong to different mating strains, one of which is called the "plus" (+) strain, and the other the "minus" (−) strain. One or more cells of each mycelial strain fuses with cells of the opposite type to form a so-called **secondary mycelium** that contains both types of nuclei. (The original mycelia are called **primary mycelia**.) The secondary mycelium might continue to grow independently of the primary mycelia, but sooner or later will develop into the fruiting body. This response is again caused by complex and unknown environmental effects, but seems to occur in the following way.

The secondary mycelium accumulates into a small heap which ultimately forms the **primordium**. The primordium can be found within or on the surface of the substrate and is not more than two millimeters in diameter. The time required for development of the primordium is quite variable — anywhere from one day to three weeks depending on the species and/or environmental factors. Ultimately, the primordium enlarges into a macroscopically visible, usually round mass of interwoven hyphae called a **button**. The button is most often found just protruding out of the substrate and can vary is size. I have seen buttons of *Mycena lilacifolia* which were no larger than 1/32nd of an inch in diameter, as well as buttons of *Amanita calyptroderma* that were six inches in diameter!

If the button is cut lengthwise into halves, the following structures can be seen. The **universal veil** is a cottony roll of mycelium that completely (universally) covers the button. The **gill cavities** contain tissue that will become the gills, structures on which the spores are borne. In the case of *Amanita* and many other mushrooms, the gill cavity is covered by another layer of tissue, at this time almost indistinguishable from surrounding layers, called the **partial veil**. The button tissue above the gill cavities will develop into the **pileus** (cap) and the part between the cavities will develop into the **stipe** (stalk).

The button grows into the mature fruiting body in two stages. (See figure 1, page 8) First, the button increases in height, due mostly to elongation of the tissue between the gill cavities. This results in a rupturing of the universal veil, with the cap and the stalk becoming visibly distinct parts of the mushroom. The rupturing of the universal veil may leave pieces or **remnants** of the veil (abbreviated u.v.) on the surface of the pileus or at the base of the stipe. On the pileus, the remnant may be a **single patch**, or various kinds of **warts**. The remnant of the universal veil attached to the base of the stipe is called a **volva** (cup). At this point the gills are still not visible in the example we are using because they are covered by the partial veil, which stretches from the apex of the stipe to the margin of the pileus. (The partial veil is abbreviated as p.v.)

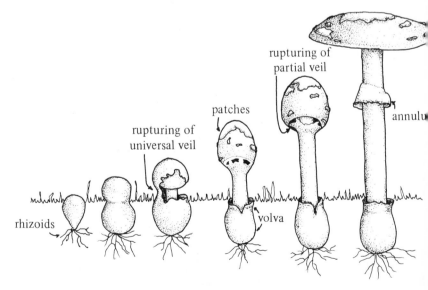

rupturing of
partial veil

patches

annulu

rupturing of
universal veil

rhizoids

volva

FIGURE 1: Development of *Amanita*

The second stage of mushroom growth emphasizes lateral development of the pileus resulting in expansion of the cap, but little if any increase in height of stipe. Due to the lateral growth, the partial veil is ruptured. In *Amanita*, the rupturing occurs all around the pileal margin, leaving a skirt-like patch called the **annulus** (ring) attached to the stalk. The **lamellae** (gills) are now visible on the undersurface of the pileus. Lining all surfaces of the gills are cells called **basidia**, which at maturity bear the **spores** (sometimes referred to more specifically as basidiospores). The function of the mushroom is to produce these spores which are liberated from the basidia and develop into another generation of hyphae.

The vast majority of fungi producing fleshy fruiting bodies belong to the class *Basidiomycetes*, so-named because of the production of basidiospores. Some, however, belong to the class *Ascomycetes*, which differ in having the spores (called **ascospores**) borne within a sac called an **ascus**. The difference between these two modes of bearing spores is illustrated in Figure 2. Among the most familiar of the Ascomycetes that produce fleshy fruiting bodies are the morels and their relatives. This book will consider only the Basidiomycete mushrooms.

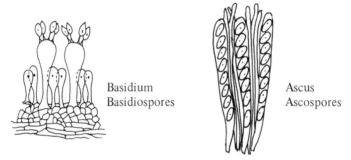

Basidium
Basidiospores

Ascus
Ascospores

FIGURE 2: Basidia and Asci

In order to identify fungi, one must be able to understand the features used for this purpose. Since the mycelium of the various species of fungi are so similar to one another the features of the fruiting body are used exclusively for those fungi that form this structure.

Almost every conceivable feature of the fruiting body has been used to identify the various species: macroscopic features, features visible only with the aid of a microscope, the reaction of the fruiting body to various chemical reagents, and even the detection of special compounds using paper chromatography. Obviously, some features are more easily used, and give more useful information than others. The novice will be able to tell which mushrooms are poisonous and which are edible by learning no more than **spore color** and **macroscopic characteristics**, and this book is designed to teach him how to accomplish this.

HOW TO USE THIS BOOK

In my opinion an amateur learns to identify mushrooms well by becoming very good at recognizing features. *After* recognizing features and *after* correlating several combinations of features an amateur will be able to identify mushrooms to genus with some degree of certainty.

This book is divided into four parts. A novice at identifying mushrooms should study the chapters in order. Persons with some experience can use the chapters in any sequence they wish.

The first part discusses the macroscopic features in detail, defining terms as completely as possible and providing several line drawings as illustrative aids. In the second part the macroscopic features are arranged in various combinations to define thirteen stature types. To understand the second part, a thorough understanding of macroscopic features is an *absolute prerequisite*. The third part organizes the common genera of mushrooms into the stature types outlined in part two and differentiates the genera within one type on the basis of spore color. Obviously, to understand the charts, you must comprehend stature types which in turn is dependent on a thorough knowledge of macroscopic features. The fourth part provides the reader with a dichotomous key to the genera of mushrooms using only macroscopic features and gives references in standard "How to Know Mushroom" books available most anywhere.

I. PART ONE

A. MEASUREMENTS OF THE FRUITING BODY

All measurements should be taken in millimeters and centimeters and sufficient measurements should be taken so that the following ratios can be calculated: pileus width/pileus height; lamella length/lamella width; stipe length/stipe width at the apex or base; pileus context/stipe width at the apex. Comparisons of these ratios may prove useful in **Aspect** determining the **aspect** of the fruiting body.

I find it convenient to arrange all measurements of the fruiting body in a way to allow for ratios to be easily calculated. For example . . .

Pileus:	Stipe: width	length	Lamellae: width	length	Trama:
(1)	(1)		(1)		(1)
(2)	(2)		(2)		(2)
(3)	(3)		(3)		(3)
(4)	(4)		(4)		(4)

B. COLOR

The colors exhibited by fleshy fungi are as varied as those found in flowers ranging from pure white to pink to reds of all shades. But yellows, yellow browns, orange-browns, and reddish-browns are the most common. Blue-grays and various shades of black are relatively uncommon, and when encountered are usually vividly remembered.

Common terms for colors tend to be used differently by different people, and since the color range of a mushroom is important in species descriptions, term used to describe colors must be applied uniformly. Numerous color standard and guides have been devised, and whenever possible, one of these standard should be used when describing the color of a mushroom.

Color is often affected by the age of the fruiting body and the environment

Therefore, always note the color ranges of young and old mushrooms of one type. In your color description, also note the condition under which the colors were described (e.g. in sunlight immediately after collecting; under artificial light; at night; 8 hours after collecting; etc.)

1. Shape of the spore bearing layer

Fungi with fleshy fruiting bodies are grouped within the Basidiomycetes on the basis of the shape of the layer which bears the basidiospores — these are as follows:

A. Fleshy with spores borne on gills — the gilled fungi or commonly called Mushrooms (Agarics).

B. Fleshy with spores borne on blunt ridges or wrinkles — the Chanterelles.

C. Fleshy with spores borne in pores or tubes — the Boletes.

D. Tough to woody with spores borne in pores or tubes — the Polypores.

E. Fleshy to tough with spores borne on teeth or spines — the Teeth or Spine Fungi.

F. Like Coral — with spores all around solitary or clustered finger-like branches — the Coral Fungi.

G. Flesh to tough — with spores borne on a smooth to bumpy surface — the Smooth or Resupinate Fungi.

The following features can be used for almost all fungi with fleshy basidiocarps; however they are used most often with those that have gills.

C. CHARACTERS OF THE PILEUS.

1. Size

Size is variable and usually correlated with the width of the stipe and thickness of the pileal flesh. A species with a broad pileus usually has a thick stipe and thick flesh. Size can sometimes be used to separate species in different genera. For example, *Crinipellis piceae* has a pileus up to 2 mm broad and *Agaricus diminutivus* has a pileus measuring from 5 to 15 mm across. On other occasions it may be used to separate species within one genus — *Boletus satanus* with a pileus from 75–325 mm broad could not xbe confused with *Boletus piperatus* with a cap up to 50 mm broad. Size is most often used, therefore, as a "negative" feature; that is, a way of eliminating certain species from consideration. But by itself, cap size is rarely, if ever, used to positively identify a mushroom species.

When taking size measurements of the pileus, measure at the point of widest diameter and greatest height.

2. Shape of Pileus

a. SIDE VIEW (Plates 1 and 2).

The shape of the cap is characteristic for given species of mushrooms, but only within broad limits. Therefore, a range of shapes, describing both young and old basidiocarps, should be used rather than an absolute shape.

These various shapes of the pileus can be arranged in a continuum in which the cap can be thought to expand laterally while at the same time appear to become shorter in height. (see Plate 1) The shape having a relatively small pileal width compared to height is called **conic** (e.g. the pileal shape of *Hygrophorus conicus*); usually the margin is straight. If the margin flares out and the apex of the cap is not as sharply pointed as in the conic shape, the cap is called **campanulate** (e.g. the narrowly campanulate pileus of *Panaeolus campanulatus*) because it has the appearance of a bell. One of the most commonly encountered pileal shapes is one that has the appearance of an inverted bowl, i.e. is regularly rounded. This is called **convex**. The width of a convex cap is normally greater than its height. If the height is greater than the width, but the cap is still regularly rounded, the term **parabolic** is used. One of the greatest extremes of a parabolic cap is found in many species of *Coprinus* in which the cap resembles a darning egg. Most convex caps continue to enlarge laterally with age, causing the width/height ratio to increase. Often this results in the cap appearing almost flat, a shape called **plane** or **applanate** (e.g. the pileal shape of *Crepidotus applanatus*[1]). Finally, with age and usually also correlated with loss of water, the margin of the cap becomes turned upward, a shape called **uplifted**.

Conic (Pl. 1B)

Campanulate (Pl. 1C)

Convex (Pl. 1A)

Parabolic (Pl. 1D,E)

Plane (= applanate) (Pl. 1F)

Uplifted (Pl. 1G)

Descriptions of the side view of the cap must take into account not only the overall outline of the pileus, but also whether or not there is a protrusion or a cavity at the apex of the cap. (see Plate 2) A protrusion, or bump at this position is called an **umbo**, and pilei that possess this structure are called **umbonate** (e.g. pileus of *Suillus umbonatus*).

Umbonate
Broadly umbonate (Pl. 2B)

The umbo can be sharply pointed, called **acute** (e.g. the umbo of *Cortinarius acutus*); or it can be rounded, termed **broadly umbonate**.

Acutely umbonate (Pl. 2A)
Cuspidate

Additionally, the umbo can be sharply delineated but rather elongated, which is called **cuspidate** (e.g. the umbo of *Entoloma cuspidatum*), or the umbo can be sharply delineated but not elongated, making the pileus appear breast-shaped, known as **mammilate** or **papillate** (e.g. the umbo of *Nolanea papillata*).

---

[1] Often, generic or specific names of fungi are derived from the same term that describes an obvious macroscopic feature of the fruiting body. When this occurs, we have included the species name in parentheses that shows the use of the term.

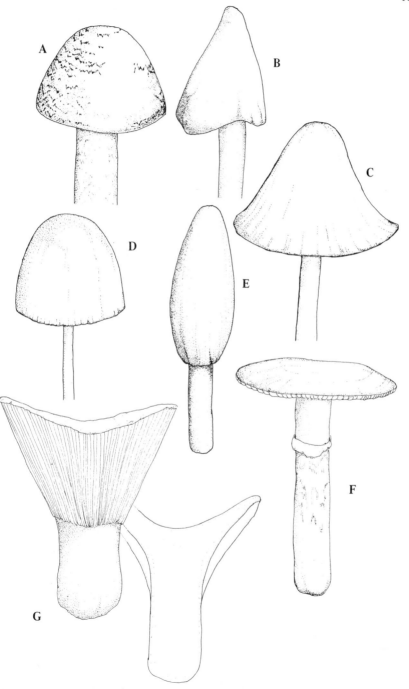

PL. 1 **Pileal Shape A.** convex, **B.** conic, **C.** campanulate, **D.** broadly parabolic, **E.** narrowly parabolic, **F.** plane, **G.** uplifted.

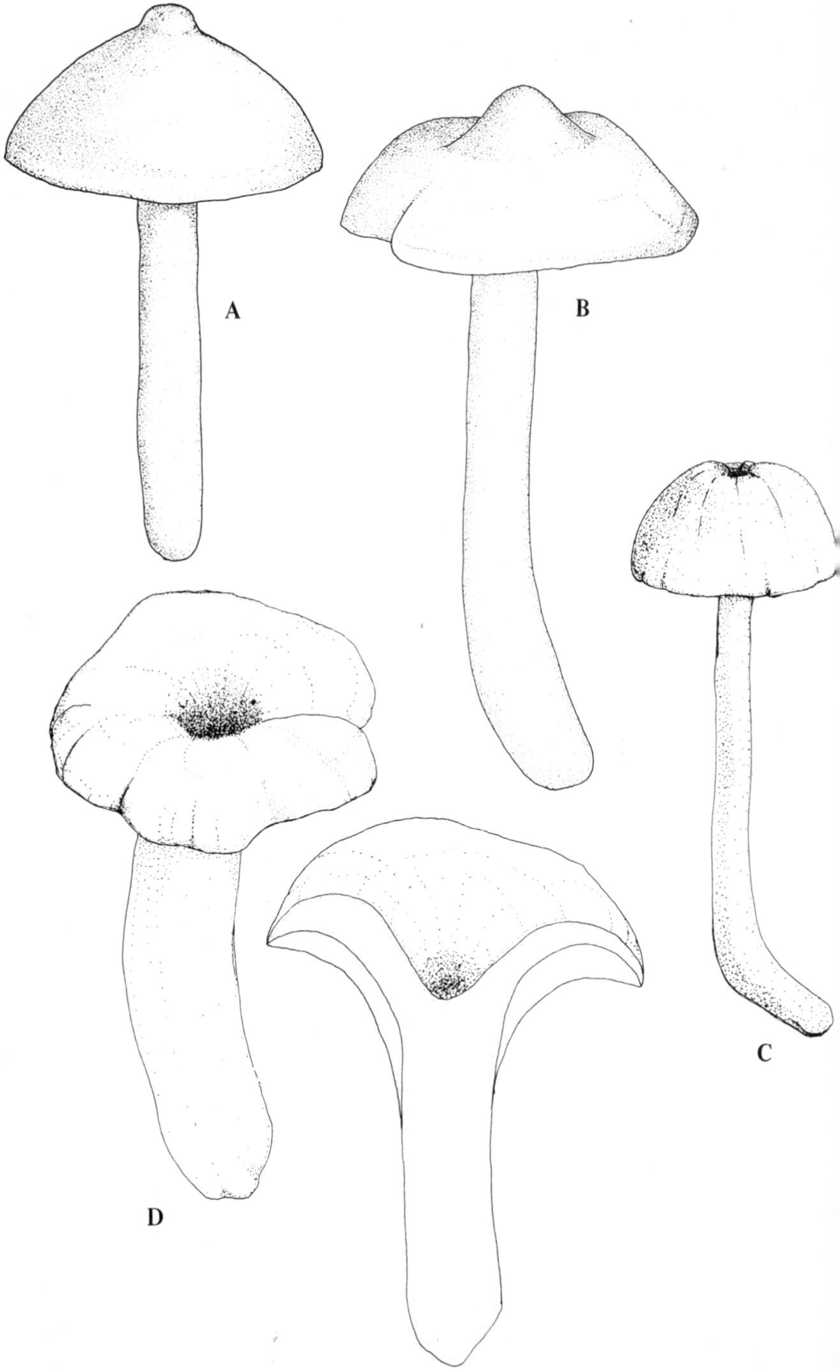

PL. 2. **Depressed & Umbonate Pilei A.** mammilate (umbo), **B.** broadly umbonate, **C.** shallowly depressed, **D.** deeply depressed.

The opposite condition from a bump is the development of a depression in the center of the pileus. The shape here is called **depressed** and is often correlated with uplifting of the pileal margin. The cap can be **shallowly depressed** or **deeply depressed**.

Shallowly depressed (Pl. 2C)
Deeply depressed (Pl. 2D)

The depression might be so deep as to resemble a funnel, called **infundibuliform** (e.g. the pileus of *Clitocybe infundibuliformis/Cantharellus infundibuliformis*). The depression might be of small diameter, **narrowly depressed**, or of large diameter, **broadly depressed**.

Infundibuliform

Narrowly depressed
Broadly depressed

In some mushrooms, an umbo occurs in the depression, a condition referred to as **umbilicate** (e.g. of the pileus of *Clitocybe umbilicatum*).

Umbilicate

b. SHAPE WHEN LOOKING DOWN ON THE PILEUS (top view).

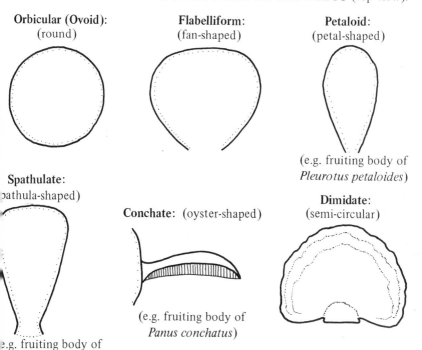

Orbicular (Ovoid): (round)

Flabelliform: (fan-shaped)

Petaloid: (petal-shaped)

(e.g. fruiting body of *Pleurotus petaloides*)

Spathulate: (spathula-shaped)

Conchate: (oyster-shaped)

Dimidate: (semi-circular)

(e.g. fruiting body of *Panus conchatus*)

(e.g. fruiting body of *Spathularia spathularis*)

FIGURE 3: Shape of Pileus

3. Color of Pileus

Color is discussed on page 10, but the following special points about color of the cap should be noted.

1. Note the color of the pileus at different ages. Often young fruiting bodies change color with age.

2. Observe the color of the disc (central region of the cap) and of the margin

Unicolorous

If the cap is uniformly colored, it is **unicolorou** (e.g. the pileus of *Galerina unicolor*).

In some cases these two regions are differentl colored, in which case the cap is said to b

Bicolorous

bicolorous (e.g. the stipe of *Nolanea bicoloripes*)

3. Notice any color changes due to bruising or simply rubbing the pilea surface.

4. Textured caps may show complex coloring. Note whether the backgrounc color of the cap is different from the color of the fibrils or squamules.

4. Margin of Pileus

The features of the pileal margin fall roughly into three general categories those dealing with the shape of the margin as seen from side view when the ca is cut in half; those features seen from top view, looking down on the pileus; an those dealing with the surface of the pileal margin.

a. SHAPE OF MARGIN (as seen in cross section) (Plate 3)

From this view, the margin of a mushroom cap may vary from complete unexpanded to completely expanded. If the margin is rolled inward so it poin

Inrolled (Pl 3A)

towards itself, it is called **inrolled** or **involute** (e. the pileal margin of *Paxillus involutus*).

Incurved (Pl. 3B)

It might be curved in less, pointing to the gill which is called **incurved**.

Decurved (= straight) (Pl. 3C)

It might be more or less parallel or pointing t the stipe, termed **decurved**, or **straight**.

Plane (Pl. 3D)

As the pileus expands, the margin usually b comes pulled upwards to become **plane** (approx mately perpendicular to stipe) or pointed upwar

Upturned (= **uplifted**) (Pl. 3E)

called **upturned**, or **uplifted**. It should be obvio that the margin in side view varies radically wi age hence these features should be described as a range, and not absolutely. / example of a typical description would be, "incurved to decurved when youn becoming decurved to plane, or at times even uplifted with age."

b. SHAPE OF MARGIN (surface view). (Figure 4)

The pileal margin of a young mushroom begi

Entire

as a perfect circle, a condition known as **entire**. the mushroom gets older the margin usually b comes interrupted to various degrees. If the int ruptions are regular, like the edge of a scallop, t

Crenate (= **scalloped**) (Fig. 4A)

margin is said to be **crenate**, or **scalloped** (regula wavy).

Crisped (= **crenulate**) (Fig. 4B)

If the margin is finely wavy, it is called **crisp** or *crenulate*; if broadly wavy, it is termed **undul**

Undulating (Fig. 4C)

ing (e.g. the fruiting body of the *Ascomycete, R zina undulata*).

Eroded (Pl. 4A)

Rimose

Appendiculate
(Pl. 4B,C,)

If the interruptions are irregular, the margin is referred to as **eroded**. (see Plate 4) If the interruptions are in the form of splits which run radially toward the pileal disc, the margin is said to be **rimose**. This term is also used when describing the surface of the cap. The pileal margin of a few species has patches or pieces of the partial veil attached to it. This is called **appendiculate** (e.g. the pileal margin of *Psathyrella appendiculata*).

A) Crenate   B) Crisped   C) Undulating

FIGURE 4: Shape of Pileal Margin (Surface View)

c. SURFACE OF MARGIN

Often the margin of the pileus appears to have lines of varying lengths oriented radially, similar to spokes of a wheel. The lines or striations might

Translucent-striate
(= pellucid)

Striate (= pectinate)

Sulcate

Plicate-striate

Tuberculate-striate

represent an image of gills seen through the top of a wet pileus, a condition known as a **translucent-striate** (or **pellucid**) (e.g. pileus of *Tubaria pellucida*) pileus. This condition is almost always associated with a hygrophanous cap. If the lines are not the image of the lamellae, but are part of the cap itself, the margin is called **striate** (e.g. the pileus of *Inocybe striata* or if small striae then the pileus of *Laccaria striatula*). A striated margin is ordinarily associated with a wavy margin shape, as seen in top view.

If the lines form definite grooves, the margin is **sulcate** (e.g. the pileal margin of *Lentinus sulcatus*).

There may be folds between the striae, a condition known as **plicate-sulcate** (e.g. pileus of *Conocybe plicatella*).

If small bumps are present on the striae, the margin is called **tuberculate-striate**. These last two features are frequently found in species of *Russula*.

18

PL. 3. **Pileal Margins (section view) A.** inrolled, **B.** incurved, **C.** decurved, **D.** plane, **E** upturned.

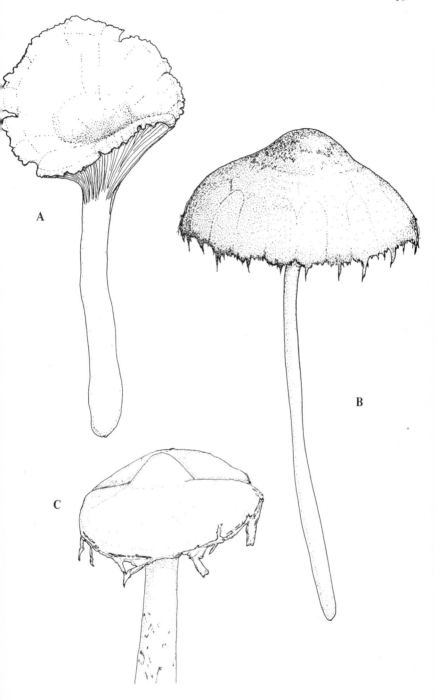

PL. 4. **Pileal Margin (surface view) A.** eroded, **B., C.** appendiculate

5. Surface of Pileus

The description of the surface of the cap is emphasized strongly by investigators in distinguishing species. The different-looking surfaces of various kinds of fleshy fungi reflect differing manners of development from the button stage and thus reveal fundamental and important differences in the fungi. Consequently, the student should learn to pay particular attention to this character when attempting to identify the fleshy fungi.

The type of pileal surface can be more intimately seen by looking at a sectioned pileus under high magnification. The system of hyphae which comprise the surface is called the **pileipellis** (or the **cuticle**). All surfaces of a fruiting body except the spore-bearing surface have a cuticle. Professional agaricologists (those who study mushrooms) often emphasize the type of cuticle possessed by a fungus as much or more than the the spore-bearing surface have a cuticle possessed by a fungus as much or more than the nature of the surface when differentiating among similar species. Here, the cuticle will be considered a microscopic character and therefore not within our scope, but students should remember that the surface (a macroscopic character) is determined by the nature of the cuticle (a microscopic character). The same system of hyphae is involved in both; the difference is only in how closely one looks at the structure.

Pileipellis (= cuticle)

Fruiting body surfaces have many characteristics, and they are often difficult to describe. The multiplication of terms designed to describe these surface properties is probably greater than for any other feature, and has resulted in bewildering array of adjectives that makes understanding this feature a formidable task. The following pages define some fifty-five terms that can be applied to pileal surfaces.

To make this section more understandable, we have tried to illustrate as many terms as possible with line drawings. Some of the features, however, can only be properly demonstrated with photographs. It is hoped that a future edition of this volume will include such photographs.

A final word about terms. Nature has provided a whole set of features. Man, in attempting to describe these features, erects terms to signify the various features, the extremes of which are fairly easy to understand. But the natural variation is usually continuous, and it is the area between the extremes that it is difficult to express in words. It is these middle areas where additional terms proliferate. Understanding the manner in which terms evolve might make learning them a bit easier.

a. SHININESS OF PILEAL SURFACE

Shiny (= lucidus)

Dull

Silky (= sericeous)

The surface can be **shiny** or **lucidus**, as if it were polished (e.g. the pileus of *Nolanea lucida*) or it can be **dull**, lacking a luster. A condition more or less between these terms is describing the surface as **silky** as if it were made of silk. Another word meaning silky is **sericeous** (e.g. the stipe of *Nolanea sericea*).

b. WETNESS OF PILEAL SURFACE

Dry (= arid)

The surface of the cap is called **dry** or **arid** (e.g. *Phaeomarasmius aridus*) if it feels as if it has no moisture in it at all. The exact opposite of dry is when the pileal surface has a heavy coating of gooey material on it resulting from the absorption of so much water by the surface that it has the consistency of liquid glue or jelly. Such a surface is called **glutinous** (e.g. the veil of *Gomphidus glutinosus*) if it is like liquid glue, or **gelatinous** if it is jelly-like. All of the remaining terms listed here describe situations between the two above extremes.

Glutinous
Gelatinous

Moist

Moist if the surface feels wet but does not fit any of the following categories.

Lubricous (= oily)

Lubricous if the surface feels slippery as if it is covered with a layer of oil or cream (e.g. the fruiting body of the *Ascomycete, Leotia lubrica*, or the pileus of *Pholiota lubrica*).

The terms **tacky**, **subviscid** and **viscid** refer to different degrees of stickiness of a pileal surface. A **viscid** (e.g. the pileus of *Chroogomphus viscidus*) surface is one in which the hyphae have absorbed water and the walls of the hyphae have begun to gelatinize (to form a type of gluten), or to become partly dissolved in water. Such a surface feels sticky to the touch (touch is the most reliable of the field tests for viscidity). Another field indicator of viscidity is the accumulation of debris on the pileal surface. **Subviscid** refers to a very slightly sticky surface (e.g. the pileal surface of *Psilocybe subviscida*), whereas **tacky** is an infrequently used term meaning less sticky than subviscid.

Viscid

Subviscid

Tacky

c. HYGROPHANOUS NATURE OF PILEAL SURFACE

In many mushrooms, when the pileal surface dries out it may change color sharply from what it was while moist. This condition is called **hygrophanous**. The process may take as long as half a day, or only a few minutes. In the latter case, unless the investigator is aware of the hygrophanous condition, the color change as well as other moisture-related features (such as a translucent-striate margin) may be overlooked.

Hygrophanous

d. TEXTURE OF PILEAL SURFACE

The surface texture of the cap can vary in essentially two ways. The first is the degree of wrinkling, splitting or pitting; and the second is the degree of association of the hyphae which make up the surface. In the first case, the property results from the way the hyphae are layered **below the cuticle**. The second group of features result from varying types of associations of the hyphae which make up the cuticle (= pileipellis).

i. Degree of Wrinkling, Splitting or Pitting

Smooth

Scrobiculate

Alveolate

Lacunose

Rimose

Lacinate

Areolate

Rivulose

Rugulose
Corrugate (= rugose)

If a pileus has no cracks, wrinkles or pits, it is called **smooth**. Otherwise, it can be one or a combination of the following.

I. **Pitted** — the pits or depressions can be shallow, a condition called **scrobiculate** (e.g. the stipe apex of *Lactarius scrobiculatus*), or deep, the pores of which are called **alveolate** (e.g. the pores of *Favolus alveolaris*). If the pits are very deep surrounded by ridges, the surface is called **lacunose** (e.g. the stalk of the Ascomycete *Helvella lacunosa*) (Fig. 12 P. 58).

II. **Split** or **Cracked** — the surface can be split usually in a radial manner, with the splits normally extending through the cuticle. In this case the pileus is called **rimose** (e.g. the pileal surface of *Inocybe rimosa*). If the splits and cracks are deep cutting the surface into rather large segments, the condition is called **lacinate** (e.g. the branches of *Hericium lacinatum*). If the surface gets torn into shreds or splits are irregular and result in the formation of block-like areas like those formed when a mud flat dries up, the condition is said to be **areolate** (e.g. *Gymnopilus areolatus*).

III. **Wrinkled with lines** — the surface might have lines shaped like a river and its tributaries, a condition called **rivulose** (e.g. *Clitocybe rivulosa*). If the cap is irregularly finely wrinkled, it is called **rugulose** (e.g. the pileus of *Lepiota rugulosa*). If coarsely wrinkled or ridged, it is called **rugose** or **corrugate** (e.g. the pileal surface of *Cortinarius corrugatus* or *Pholiota rugosa* or the annulus of *Stropharia rugoso-annulata*). Or the wrinkles might be as conspicuous as folds, which is termed **gyrose** (e.g. the pileus of the Ascomycete, *Gyromitra* spp.).

23

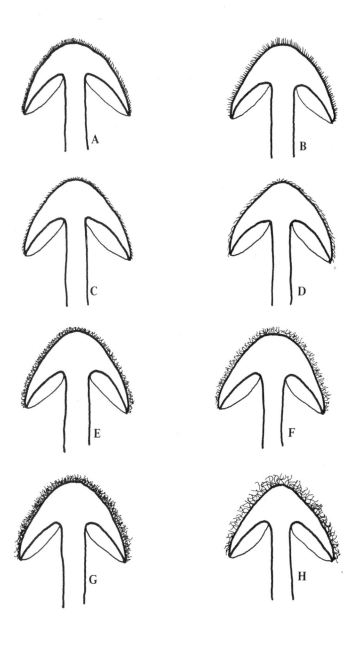

PL. 5. **Pileal Surface A.** velutinous, **B.** hispid, **C.** pubescent **D.** canescent, **E.** floccose, **F.** tomentose, **G.** matted fibrillose, **H.** villose.

ii. Degree of Hyphal Association on Pileal Surface. (Plate 5, 6)

The hyphae of the outer surface of the pileus can be oriented and associated with one another in different ways to form easily observable surface textures. The pileus might be perfectly "bald", in which case it is called *glabrous*. This is contrasted with a surface consisting of erect, stiff hairs that is called *hispid*, or a surface with erect, stiff scales (squamules), called *scabrous*. All other terms used here reflect intermediate conditions.

Glabrous
Glabrescent

Atomate

Micaceous

Glabrous — bald, even, smooth, like a waxed surface. Sometimes the term **glabrescent** is used, which means "becoming glabrous", or somewhat glabrous. A glabrous pileus may have some apparent texture which is more or less of an optical illusion, and is dependent on light reflection. If it appears as though covered by minute, shining particles it is called **atomate** (e.g. *Psathyrella atomata*). If it looks as though it is covered by glistening mica-like particles, it is called **micaceous** (e.g. the pileal surface of *Coprinus micaceus*).

The hyphae of the pileal surface may be associated, grouped or agglutinated (stuck together) with each other. The result is that the surface appears to be covered with powder, granules, fibrils, hairs, or scales. If the fibrils, etc. are present on young specimens, but disappear in older forms, they are said to be **superficial**. If they are lasting present on young and old specimens alike, they are called **innate**. The superficial particles are usually the remains of the partial veil or universal veil or both, whereas the innate structures derive from an intergrowth of the hyphae in the pileal cuticle (= pileipellis). The amount of hyphal association and the manner of the ssociation (whether laterally stuck together, or apically, or both) is the important factor in differentiating the following terms.

Superficial

Innate

Pruinose (= pulverulent)

Furfuraceous

Granulose (= granular)

If the pileus is covered with a fine powder as if it were sprinkled with a very fine flour, it is called **pruinose** or **pulverulent** (e.g. the veil of *Pulveroboletus* or the stipe of *Russula pulverulenta* or the pileus of *Lepiota pulveracea*). If the powder is bran-like in size and the pileus appears scurfy (composed of dry external scales of cuticle, like dandruff), it is said to be **furfuraceous** (e.g. the pileus of *Tubaria furfuracea*). If the powder is larger yet, like grains of salt, the surface is called **granulose** or **granular** (e.g. the pileal surface of *Cystoderma granulosum*).

When the hyphae agglutinate laterally on the pileal cuticle, they form a texture with visible filaments or fibrils. A cap with

PL. 6. **Pileal Surface A.** recurved squamulose, **B.** appressed squamulose.

Fibrillose a surface of this kind is called **fibrillose** (e.g. the pileus of *Leccinum fibrillosum*). If this condition is combined with a split surface, it is referred to as **Rimose-fibrillose** **rimose-fibrillose**.

Fibrils appressed (flattened) on the surface are **Appressed-fibrillose** termed **appressed-fibrillose**. If the appressed fibrils appear as if they are mere streaks, the surface is **Virgate** called **virgate** (streaked) (e.g. the pileal surface of *Tricholoma virgatum*). The fibrils might appear parallel to the surface, but not flattened. A number of terms are applied here depending on the appearance of the fibrils as seen *en masse*. For example, the pileal surface is called **downy-** **Downy-fibrillose** **fibrillose** when the fibrils form a downy layer. If it **Canescent (= hoary)** is densely downy, it is called **canescent** or **hoary** **(Pl. 5D)** (e.g. *Hygrophorus canescens*). When the fibrils have the appearance of cotton flannel, the term **Floccose** (Pl. 5E) **floccose** is normally used. Sometimes this same **Downy-wooly** property is called **downy-wooly** to denote a condition intermediate between downy-fibrillose **Tomentose** (Pl. 5F) and the next term, **tomentose**, which refers to fibrils that are densely matted and wooly, like a woolen blanket (e.g. the pileal surface of *Chroo- gomphus tomentosus*). A condition close to tom- entose where the fibrils are matted and inter- **Matted-fibrillose** (Pl. 5G) woven, appearing like felt is called **matted- fibrillose**.

The fibrils can also be more or less perpendicular to the pileal surface, making the surface look like it is made of distinct hairs. The stiffness of the hairs can vary from weak to stiff, and the surface can feel like velvet or like a bristle brush, respectively. If the hairs are weak and more or less flexible either **Velutinous** (Pl. 5A) of two terms can be used. **Velutinous** refers to a surface where the hairs are compact, short, firm and soft (velvety) (e.g. the pileal surface of *Psathyrella velutina* or the stipe of *Collybia velutipes*). If the hairs are rather long and weak, it **Villose** (Pl. 5H) is called **villose**. If the hairs are short, it is called **Pubescent** (Pl. 5C) **pubescent** (e.g. the pileus of *Crepidotus pub- escens*). If the hairs are stiff and rather inflexible **Hirsute** the pileal surface can be called **hirsute** (e.g. the pileal surface of *Inocybe hirsuta*). If the hairs retain a bit of flexibility resulting in a surface **Hispid** (Pl. 5B) tending to villose, the term **hispid** (e.g. *Pluteus hispidulus*) is appropriate. Sometimes the hairs are bristle-like, long and coarse and more or less oriented as if appressed either on the surface of the pileus or on the substrate at the base of the

Strigose   stipe, a condition called **strigose** (e.g. the pileal surface of *Panus strigosus*).

Agglutination of fibrils can occur at the tips of the hyphae as well as laterally. When the tips stick together, a scale is formed. A scaly surface is called **squamose**

Squamose
Squamulose[1]
(e.g. the pileal surface of *Psathyrella squamosa*) (or, if the scales are small, **squamulose**[1]). This condition may result from splitting or tearing of the surface as well as agglutination. As with fibrils, scales may be flattened (appressed), giving

Appressed-squamulose
(Pl. 6B)
Imbricate-scaly
appressed-squamulose surfaces, or they may even overlap with one another, giving a surface called **imbricate-scaly** (e.g. the pileal surface of *Tricholoma imbricatum*). If the scales are erect, a series of terms are applied to signify the degree of erectness. They are:

Recurved squamulose
(Pl. 6A)
recurved squamulose — the tips of the scales are erect and turn backwards.

Squarrose
squarrose — the scales are upright, particularly in the area of the center of the pileus (e.g. the pileal surface of *Pholiota squarrosa*). At times this is used in a similar way to scabrous (see Smith, 1949) or as recurved squamulose (see Snell and Dick, 1957).

Punctate-squamulose
punctate-squamulose — the surface is dotted with minute scales or points.

Scabrous
Scabrulose[1]
scabrous (scabrulose[1]) — the surface is rough to the touch due to large scales or points. This term is often used for the stipe apex of *Leccinum* (e.g. the stipe apex of *Leccinum scabrum*).

CAUTION! When describing the surface of the fruiting body, the conditions of the surface may vary widely with age, maturity, weather, time, etc. Therefore, collect as many specimens as possible at all stages of development and under all conditions being sure to relate data with all notes taken.

6. Flesh of Pileus

The following features of the pileal flesh (also referred to as *trama*) are sporadically emphasized in descriptions of fleshy fungi and should be noted when describing a fruiting body.

1. Color and color changes.
2. Thickness — measured in millimeters, at the margin and at the center.
3. Consistency — whether it is soft, hard, turgid (full of water), fragil or tough.
4. Taste and odor.

Often the suffix *-ulose* is added to a term if a condition is almost but not exactly like the parent term, or if the condition is a smaller version of the parent term.

Taste and odor are common features used by agaricologists to distinguish among closely related species. Many of the terms used to define different odors are used differently by different people. This is due not only to lack of precision and uniformity in the descriptive terms commonly used, but also to the fact that individual human perceptions in taste are variable. Just as some people are color blind, others are "taste blind" or "odor blind". (from Smith, 1949)

When one smells a small piece of crushed pileal flesh, the hands and fingers should be absolutely clean. Some of the more useful odors are: **unpleasant** or **disagreeable** (check all specimens to make sure you are not smelling a putrefying mushroom), **fragrant** and pleasant to sweet; (e.g. the odor of *Clitocybe fragrans*), **anise-like** (or like licorice), **raphanoid** (e.g. the odor of *Cortinarius raphanoides*) (like a radish), **fabaceous** (bean-like) (e.g. *Leptonia fabaceola*), and **farinous**, which is like the odor of fresh meal. Any of these latter categories can be applied to pleasant or unpleasant, depending on the individual.

Taste is as important as odor in describing mushrooms, and just as difficult to describe. One important point here is that taste is not indicative of edibility! Some species have pleasant tastes but are poisonous. *Agaricus albolutescens* has an anise odor, but is potentially toxic. *Agaricus placomyces* has an unpleasant (creosote) odor, but some people can eat it. Some of the more common categories of taste are **mild**, **peppery** or **acrid** (leaving a burning sensation on the tongue (e.g. the taste of *Lacturius piperatus*), and **farinous**. Often the taste can be mild at first, but become distinctive after awhile. In this case the taste is said to be **latent** (e.g. *Lactarius rufus*).

7. Presence or Absence of Latex

The flesh of the pileus, as well as the gills, sometimes exudes a milk-like substance, or latex, when cut. Such an exudate is characteristic, for example, of species of *Lactarius*. The presence or absence of color and color changes on the gills, as well as the taste and odor of the latex should be noted.

D. CHARACTERS OF THE LAMELLAE

1. Attachment (Plate 7)

The manner in which the gills are attached to the apex of the stipe is considered an important feature when differentiating species of mushrooms. However, since it can vary with the maturity of the fruiting body, and with different environmental conditions, or even on the same fruiting body, it must be interpreted with considerable latitude. The attachment can vary from squarely on the stipe to not attached at all, or to running down the stipe.

The following terms and accompanying illustrations describe the various ways that gills attach to the stipe.

Free (Pl. 7A; Fig. 11)

Free applies to the situation where the gills do not meet the stipe at all. In this instance, a portion of the pileus can be seen as a small ring at the top of the stipe. If there is a big gap, the term **remote** is used. With age and/or dry conditions, or when the pileus is uplifted, the gills frequently pull away

Remote

Seceding

from the stipe. They are said to be **seceding**. This can be confused with the attachment mode called free, but should be easy to detect since small lines, representing the remnants of the gill, can be seen remaining on the stipe apex.

Adnexed (Pl. 7C)

Adnexed is where the gills appear as if they are attached at only a portion of their width and the resultant shape is as if a large triangular piece had been removed from that portion of the gill where it meets the stipe.

Emarginate (= abruptly adnexed) (Pl. 7B)

Emarginate applies if the gills appear sharply adnexed and the triangular piece is relatively small. Also called **abruptly adnexed**.

Notched (= sinuate) (Pl. 7D)

Notched (= sinuate) describes gills that appear as if a small notch has been taken out at the point where they meet the stipe (e.g. *Entoloma sinuatum*).

Adnate

Adnate describes the situation where the gills are more or less squarely attached to the stipe, meaning along most of the gill width (e.g. the gill attachment of *Amanita adnata* (= *Amanita gemmata*) or of *Lepiota adnatifolia*).

Arcuate-decurrent

Arcuate-decurrent describes gills shaped like a bow, curving upward and then running down the stipe for a short distance, (e.g. *Tricholoma arcuata*).

Decurrent (Pl. 7F; Fig 9)

Decurrent is the term used when the gills run down the stipe. If the distance down the stipe is relatively short, the attachment is said to be **subdecurrent**.

Subdecurrent (Pl. 7E)

2. Spacing of Gills

This is an arbitrary feature, but still useful since it gives knowledge of the overall aspect of the gills. The terms used are **crowded** if the gills are so close together such that the spaces between the gills can not be seen; **close**, then **subdistant**, if the gills are slightly more open than the closed situation, and **distant** (e.g. the gills of *Cortinarius distans*), if the gills are quite far apart. (Figure 5)

  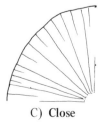 

A) **Distant**   B) **Subdistant**   C) **Close**   D) **Crowded**

FIGURE 5: Spacing of Gills

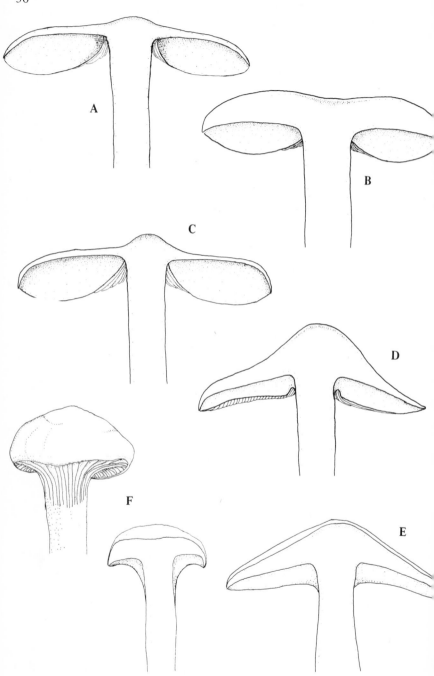

PL. 7. **Gill Attachment A.** free, **B.** emarginate (abruptly adnexed) **C.** adnexed, **D.** sinuate (notched) **E.** subdecurrent **F.** decurrent.

3. Relative Thickness of Gills

This is another arbitrary characteristic. The width is considered in relation to the size of the cap and the size of the basidiocarp in general. The terms used are:

Narrow; broad — **narrow**, for extremely thin gills; **broad**, for thick
Moderately broad — gills; **moderately broad**, for gills whose thickness is
Ventricose — intermediate between narrow and broad; **ventricose** (e.g. *Pholiota ventricosa*) referring to the gills which are swollen midway between the stipe and the margin of the pileus. It is useful to distinguish
Gill thickness — between **gill thickness** (distance between adjacent
Gill width (= gill breadth) — gills) and **gill width** (= **gill breadth**) (the relative distance from the top part of the gill where it joins the pileal context and the bottom, exposed edge of the gill).

4. Color and Color Changes of Lamellae (and Latex)

It is very important to note the color of young gills before spore maturation. This feature is used to separate many species and takes on greatest importance in the genus *Cortinarius*. The color of mature gills should be observed because this can be used to predict spore color. (*Be Careful*; all too frequently the color of mature gills is not due to the color of the spores).

5. Margin of Gills (Plate 8)

The features of the gill edge are important since unusual shapes of colors often represent the presence of sterile cells called **cystidia** that do not produce basidiospores. Most of the features described below can be easily seen with a hand lens. If the gill edge is colored differently than the face (side) of the gill, it is called **marginate** (e.g. the reddish (= rubro) gill edge of *Mycena rubromarginata*). When
Marginate — the gill edge is uninterrupted, it is referred to as
Smooth — **smooth**. If the edge is minutely torn or fringed, it
Fimbriate — is **fimbriate** (e.g. *Hygrophorus fimbratophylla*). If the tears of fringes are large so that the edge appears toothed like the edge of a saw, it is said to
Serrate (Pl. 8E) — be **serrate** or **serrulate** if the teeth are small (e.g.
Serrulate (Pl. 8F) — the gill edge of *Leptonia serrulata*). If the margin is regularly wavy like the edge of a scallop, the term
Crenate (= scalloped) (Pl. 8A,D) — **crenate** or **scalloped** is used.
Eroded (Pl. 8D) — When the waviness is irregular and the waves perhaps a bit torn, it is called **eroded**. When the waviness is more or less regular but quite small, it
Crisped (Pl. 8B) — is **crisped** (e.g. *Conocybe crispa*). A condition with
Undulating — broader waves is called **undulating**. The reader will

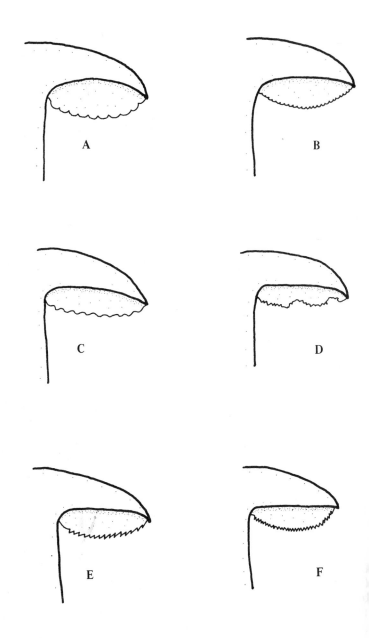

PL. 8. **Gill Margin A.** crenate, **B.** crisped, **C.** wavy, **D.** eroded, **E.** serrate, **F.** serrulate.

recall that many of these terms here applied to the gill margin were also applied earlier to the pileal margin.

6. Gill Face

The features of the face of the gill are also important since they may indicate ¿ presence of cystidia. Terms such as **pruinose** (or **pulverulent**) meaning powdery in appearance, or **pubescent** a minutely hairy appearance, are used to describe gill faces with projecting cystidia. At times, the gill face is lustrous because of thickness and being watery; it often appears as if covered with wax, a condition **Laccate (= waxed)** called **laccate** or **waxed** (e.g. the gills of *Laccaria laccata*).

7. Gill Features Observed by Viewing from Edge to Pileus

If one turns the mushroom upside down, setting it on its pileal surface and ¿ks at the gills "edge-on", some additional features are readily apparent. For example, some gills do not extend entirely from the margin to the stipe. Such gills are called **Lamellulae** **lamellulae**. Between adjacent gills there may be one set or series of lamellae extending approximately one-half to one-third the length of the gill. A second series may be present which extends between the lamellulae of the first series and the complete lamellae.

Rather than run continuously in one line, gills may divide into distinct ¿nches between the pileal margin and stipe apex. The pattern of such branching is the basis of several more terms. If the branching is irregular and sporadic, the gills are **Furcate (bifurcate)** said to be **furcate** (e.g. *Russula furcata*). If the gill divides into just two branches, whether the branches are regular or not, it is called **bifurcate**. If the branching is repeated, and each branch is to **Dichotomus** two branches of equal length, the gills are said to **(= dichotomusly** be **dichotomus**, or **dichotomusly branched** (e.g. **branched)** *Cantharellus dichotomus*).

Frequently, small gills connect the face of one gill or lamellula with the side ¿an adjacent one. This makes the entire gill area appear as if it were veined. The condition of having such interconnections is **Anastomosing** termed **anastomosing** gills. The type of branching **Intervenose (= costate)** pattern is referred to as **intervenose** or **costate** (e.g. the gills of *Entoloma subcostatum*).

E. CHARACTERISTICS OF THE STIPE

1. Size of Stipe

Measurements in millimeters should be taken of the diameter of the stipe apex, middle and base; and the length of the stipe from the attachment of the gills to the substrate.

2. Attachment of Stipe (Plate 9)

a. ATTACHMENT TO PILEUS

Central (Pl. 9A)

Lateral (Pl 9B)
Excentric

The usual pattern is for the stipe to attach in the center of the pileus, called **central**. If the attachment is at the margin of the pileus, it is called **lateral**. Any attachment intermediate between central and lateral is termed **excentric** (e.g. *Crepidotus excentricus*).

b. ATTACHMENT TO SUBSTRATE AND BASAL TOMENTUM

The most typical manner in which the stipe is attached to the substrate is by a mass of hyphae originating in the substrate and superficially running up the surface at the base of the stipe. This mass of hyphae is called the **basal tomentum**, and its relative abundance should be noted, using such terms as absent, scarce, moderate, or abundant.

Basal tomentum

Rhizoids
Rhizoidal

Strigose

Rhizomorphs

Inserted (Fig. 6)

Pseudorhiza
Radicated

At times, the hyphae at the stipe base can be large and rather distinct from one another, in which case the hyphae are called **rhizoids**, and the basal tomentum is defined as **rhizoidal** (e.g. of the white (albi-) rhizoids of *Clitocybe albirhiza*). Sometimes the hyphae are large, long, and stiff like bristles. This condition is called **strigose**. In some cases, the hyphae are cord-like and more or less elastic in consistency, and are named **rhizomorphs**. Infrequently, the stipe is completely devoid of any hyphae, rhizoids or rhizomorphs, hence is completely naked where it originates from the substrate. In this situation, the stipe is said to be **inserted**. (Figure 6)

Some mushrooms have a stipe that continues as a root-like process called a **pseudorhiza**. In this case, the stipe is said to be **radicated** (e.g. the stipe of *Collybia radicata*).

35

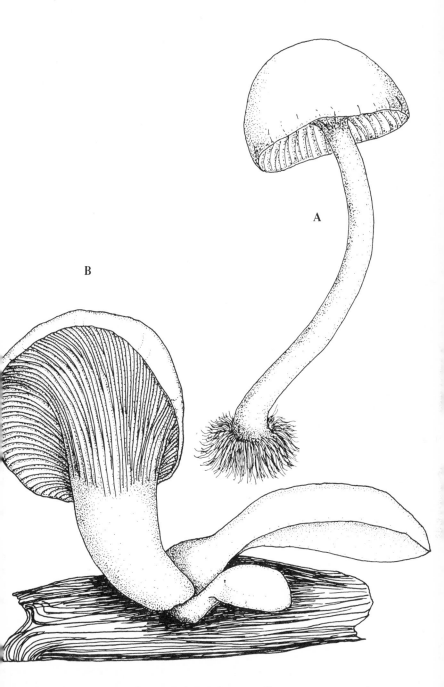

PL. 9. **Stipe Attachment A.** central, **B.** lateral.

FIGURE 6: Inserted Stipe

3. Shape of Stipe (Plate 10, 11)

a. CROSS SECTION

Terete

Compressed

Usually the stipe is perfectly round if seen from end view, a condition called **terete**. At times, however, it appears flattened, a condition called **compressed** (e.g. of the stipe of *Clitocybe compressipes*).

b. LONGITUDINAL VIEW

Equal (Pl. 10A,B)
Tapered (Pl. 10B,C,D)

Clavate (Pl. 10F)

Subclavate (Pl. 10E)
Incrassate

Bulbous (Pl. 11B)

Clavate-bulbous (Pl. 11A)

Marginate

If the stipe is of equal diameter from the apex to the base, it is called **equal**. More often than not, however, it is **tapered** in one direction or the other. If it is thickened more toward the base, a number of different terms might be applied, depending on the degree of the thickening. If it is thickened noticeably, so that the stipe has the appearance of a club, the term **clavate** (e.g. the stipe of *Clitocybe clavipes*) is used. An intermediate shape (not quite club-shaped) is termed **subclavate**; a shape not quite subclavate is called **incrassate**. If it is thickened only at the base, something like the base of a green onion, it is called **bulbous** (e.g. the stipe base of *Galerina bulbifera* and of *Cortinarius bulbosus*). An intermediate condition between bulb and club-shaped is called **clavate-bulbous**.

In a bulbous stipe, the shape of the bulb becomes an important feature. The bulb is called **marginate** if there is a distinct margin around the edge. If marginate and the upper surface is shaped like the upper surface of a saucer, it is termed

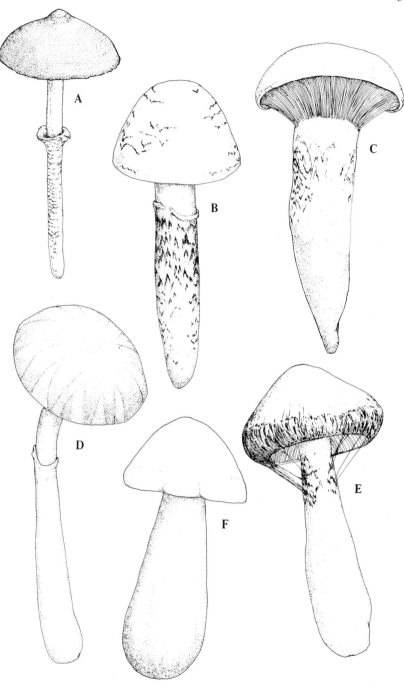

PL. 10. **Stipe Shape A.** equal, **B.** equal, slightly tapered at the base, **C.** tapered from apex to base, **D.** tapered from base to apex, **E.** subclavate, **F.** clavate.

38

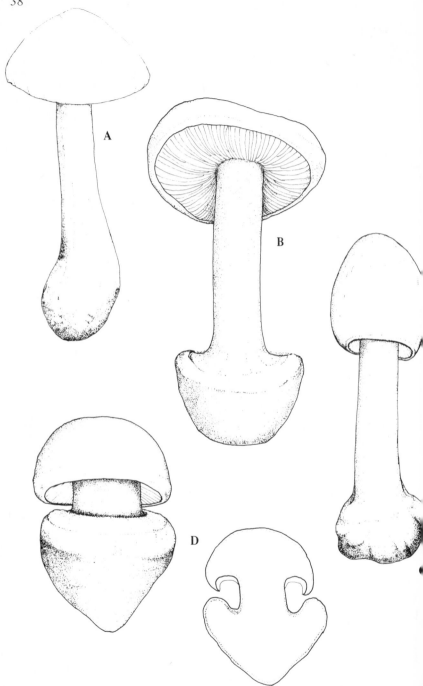

PL. 11. **Stipe Shape A.** clavate-bulbous, **B.** equal with bulbous base, **C.** equal with abrup
bulbous base, **D.** equal with marginate-depressed bulbous base.

Marginate-depressed
(Pl. 11D)

Abruptly-bulbous
(Pl. 11C)

marginate-depressed which can only be seen in sectional view. If the bulb is so sharply defined that the angle formed by the upper part of the bulb where it hits the stipe is almost a right angle it is called **abruptly-bulbous** (e.g. the stipe base of *Agaricus abruptibulbus*).

4. Surface of Stipe

The same terms used in describing the surface of the pileus can be used in escribing the surface of the stipe. Particularly important is the difference etween the surface at the apex of the stipe and that in the middle or the base. ften, this difference indicates that a veil was attached at the point where the vo surfaces are distinct from one another.

Because of the possibility of veils attached to the stipe, one should be pecially attentive regarding powder, bran-like areas, granules, fibrils, hair or scales. Note carefully whether such features are **innate**, i.e. part of the cuticle of the stipe, or are **superficial**, and can be easily removed.

Three surface features important in identifying the boletes are the following. If the stipe apex is

Glandular-dotted
(Pl. 12C)

Scabrous (Pl. 12B)

Reticulate (Pl. 12A)

dotted with what appears to be colored spots (glandules), the surface is called **glandular dotted**. If the stipe apex is roughened due to erect, pointed scales, the term **scabrous** is used. If the stipe apex has fine lines or less frequently fibrils in the form of a distinct net, the condition is a pattern of raised lines referred to as **reticulate**. (Plate 12)

The surface can also be ridged or wrinkled, with different terms used to signate the relative strength of the ridges or wrinkles. If the ridges are just fine

Longitudinal-striate

Rugulose
Rugose

Veined
(= ribbed; costate)

Canaliculate (= fluted)
Lacunose (Fig. 12)

lines, and the lines tend to be longitudinal and more or less parallel to one another, the surface is called **longitudinal striate**. If the striations or lines are interconnected and form wrinkles, the surface is called **rugulose** if finely wrinkled, or **rugose** if coarsely wrinkled (e.g. *Leccinum rugosus*). When the wrinkles are more definite and have rounded edges, they are called **veins** or **ribs**. Such surfaces are called **veined** or **ribbed** (= costate). Finally, the edges might become sharp, making the stipe appear as if it had canals or channels alternating with furrows. This sort of effect is termed **canaliculate** or **fluted** or even **lacunose**.

5. Color and Color Changes of Stipe

Note the color of young and old fruiting bodies, before and after bruising or

40

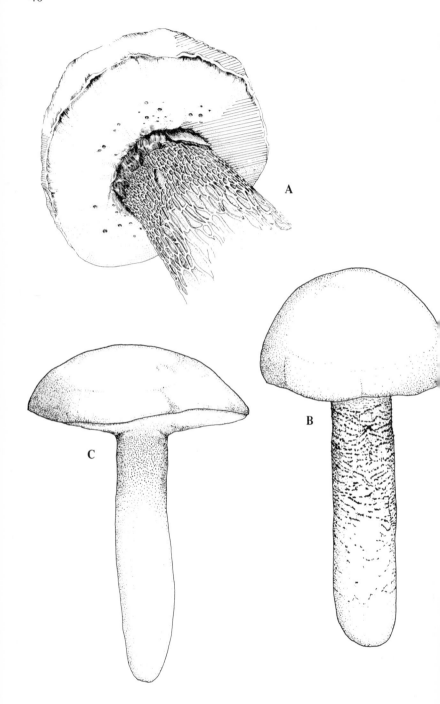

PL. 12. **Surface at the Stipe Apex A.** reticulate, **B.** punctate (scabrous) **C.** glandular dotte

rubbing. The comments on color and color changes of the pileus (page 15) apply also the the stipe.

6. Consistency of Stipe

The texture of the stipe was strongly emphasized in the past, but these distinctions are not currently considered to be quite so important. Some distinctions are useful, however, in distinguishing groups of mushrooms.

Cartilaginous　　　　　　　　　One of the common stipe textures is **cartilaginous** (e.g. the stipe of *Clitocybe cartilaginea*). Such a stipe is usually thin and breaks with a firm split when bent in two, similar to cartilage.

On occasion, a stipe will have a fibrous (see below) core, but still have a cartilaginous rind. I would characterize this stipe as cartilaginous.

Fibrous (= fleshy-fibrous)　　A **fibrous** (or **fleshy-fibrous**) stipe is usually rather thick, and when broken in two, leaves a ragged edge. In the past, size has been used to distinguish a cartilaginous from a fleshy-fibrous stipe, with the former being defined as less than 5 mm thick at the apex and the latter as being greater than 4 mm. Of course the size criterion becomes ambiguous for the many mushrooms having stipes in the neighborhood f 4-5 mm in diameter. A rule of thumb regarding this size-texture relationship is hat it applies about 75% of the time. But be careful with the other 25%.

Some other stipe texture features that are used less than the above two are:

Woody　　　　　　　　　　　　**woody**, having the texture of wood;
Corky　　　　　　　　　　　　**corky**, having the texture of cork;
Leathery (= coriaceous)　　　**leathery** (or **coriaceous**), having the texture of leather.

One of the most distinctive and therefore useful textures is a stipe that feels and breaks like chalk in the hand. When crushed, it breaks up into
Chalky　　　　　　　　　　　powder or chunks. Such a stipe is called **chalky**.

7. Flesh of Stipe

The flesh of the stipe varies from one in which the hyphae are closely packed
Solid　　　　　　　　　　　and is called **solid**, to one where the center
Hollow (= fistulose)　　　becomes empty and is called **hollows**, or **fistulose** (e.g. *Russula fistulosa*). An intermediate condition
Stuffed　　　　　　　　　　between solidand hollow is called **stuffed**.

8. Presence or Absence of Veils on Stipe

a. PARTIAL VEIL (Plate 13 & 14)

The partial veil covers the lamellae from the stipe to the margin of the pileus.

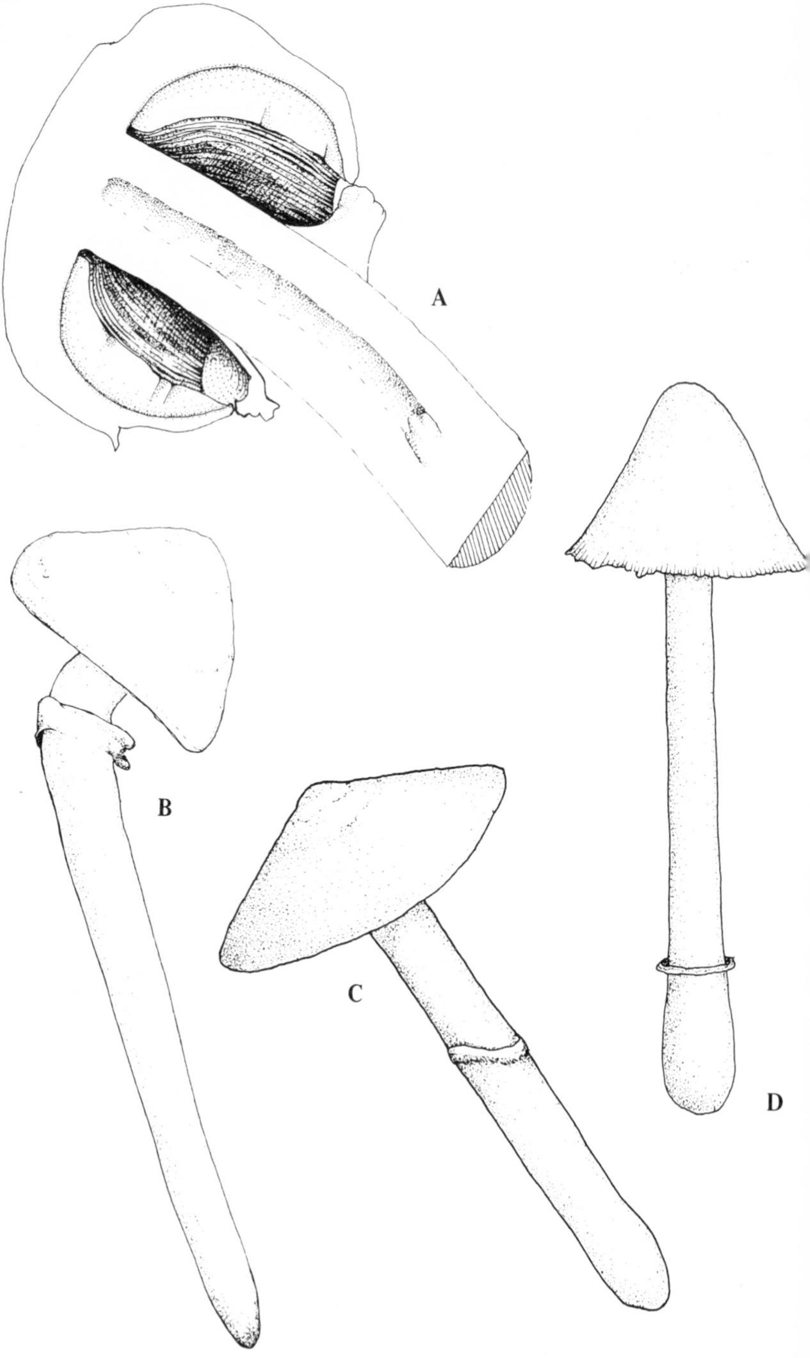

PL. 13. **Positon of Annulus A**. apical and partial veil still intact, **B**. apical (superior), central, **D**. basal (inferior).

As the cap expands, the veil breaks and remnants might be left, either on the pileal margin in the form of patches or fibrils, or on the stipe, or both. The partial veil remaining on the stipe can take either of two general forms, depending on how it ruptures. If the veil tears in a circle concentric to the stipe, the stipe will retain patches, flaps of tissue, or membranes. This sort of veil is called **membranaceous**. The ring of tissue formed by a membranous veil is called an **annulus** (ring). The other pattern is that the veil can split radially, so that the portion remaining on the stipe has the form of fibrils, often resembling a cobweb. This pattern is called **arachnoid** or a **cortina** (e.g. *Cortinarius*).

Whatever the nature of the veil as it remains on the stipe, if it is located in the top half of the stipe, it is said to be **superior** (sometimes the term *apical* is used),

Superior (= apical)
(Pl. 13A,B)
Inferior (= basal)
(Pl. 13D)
Central (Pl. 13C)

and if the lower half, it is **inferior** (or *basal*). If located approximately in the middle, the term **central** is applied.

Several terms are designed to describe the annulus, the membranous partial veil remaining on the stipe. First of all, the annulus can be either

Attached
Moveable
Double annulus (Fig. 10)
Single annulus (Pl. 14A)

attached or **moveable**. Also it may have a cottony roll of tissue on the underside, in which case it is called a **double annulus**. If the undersurface is smooth, the annulus is termed **single**.

Occasionally, the hyphae which make up the partial veil cover the entire basal portion of the stipe like a stocking, and flares out into an annulus at the apex.

Peronate (Pl. 14B)

This condition is called a **peronate** partial veil, often interpreted as a universal veil.

b. UNIVERSAL VEIL

A universal veil can be present or absent on a mushroom button. If present, remnants of the veil can be left on the pileal surface and/or around the base of the stipe after the mushroom as matured.

The universal veil as it remains around the base is called a *volva*. The main feature of the volva is whether the tissue is mostly *free* from the stipe base, or largely interwoven with the hyphae of the base and difficult to remove. The latter condition is called *adherent*. One should always correlate the volva with the type of universal veil remnants seen on the pileal surface, so that some idea can be obtained on how the veil ruptured, and for those dealing with microscopic characters, on the type of cells to expect when observing the veil microscopically.

i. Types of Free Volvas (Plate 15)

Saccate (Pl. 15B)

Membranous saccate

When the veil appears like a large bag loosely fitted around the base, the volva is termed **saccate**. If the tissue is strong and doesn't tear easily, it is called a **membranous saccate** volva. This type of volva usually remains attached to the base of the stipe when the mushroom is picked.

44

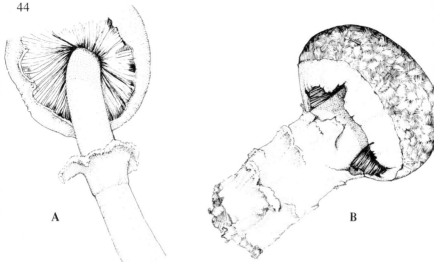

PL. 14. **Types of Partial Veils A.** single annulus, **B.** peronate (can be interpreted as a universal veil).

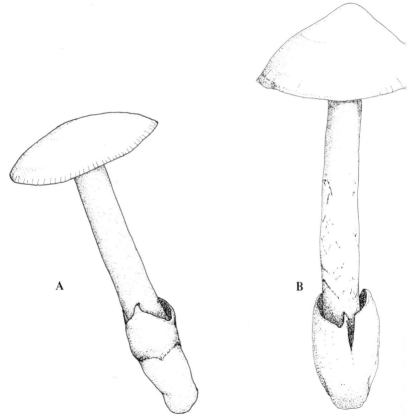

PL. 15. **Types of Universal Veils A.** constricted (adherent with a flaring margin) **B.** saccate

Fragile saccate   In some instances, the tissue making up the saccate volva is very **fragile** and is hardly adherent to the base. In this case, the veil remnants usually remain in the substrate when the mushroom is picked.

ii. Types of Adherent Volvas   (Plate 16)

Flaring (Pl. 15A)   A familiar pattern here is the **flaring** volva. It remains in one piece and is adherent along most of its length except at the top where it flares out into a loose, free layer of tissue. Similar to this is the **Circumsessile** (Pl. 16C)   **circumsessile** volva, where instead of the flare at the top as above, there is simply a tight rim of tissue. At times, the volva is so tightly adherent to the stipe base that when the stipe elongates, some of the tissue of the volva is split into rings. These rings are carried upward and form zones just above **Zoned** (Pl. 16A,D; Fig. 8) the larger part of the volva. This is called a **zoned** volva. Similar to the zoned pattern, but with scales **Scaly** (Pl. 16B)   developing in place of zones is a **scaly** volva. The most difficult kind of volva to recognize is **Powdery (= farinose)**   **powdery** or **farinose** (e.g. the veil of *Amanita farinosa*). This results when the universal veil is composed of oval cells that macroscopically give the appearance of a powdery surface.

F. GROWTH HABIT

Growth habit refers to the manner in which *numbers* of a mushroom grow in an area — whether they are widely spaced, clumped, etc. This is considered an important feature since it reveals the number and amount of mycelia involved. The various categories of growth habit are:

Solitary   **Solitary** (e.g. *Amanita solitaria*);

Scattered   **Scattered**, where the fruiting bodies are grouped one to two feet apart;

Gregarious   **Gregarious**, where they are grouped close together; and

Caespitose   **Caespitose** (e.g. *Clitocybe caespitosa*, *Cortinarius caespitosus*), where they are growing extremely close together, in fact, apparently out of the same mass. A variation of caespitose is the **Connate**   situation called **connate** (e.g. *Lyophyllum connatum*), where several stipes are grown together for quite a distance from the base upward.

G. TYPE OF FRUITING BODY ATTACHMENT (Plate 17 & Figure 7)

Normally, fruiting bodies are attached to their substrate by the stipe. This is

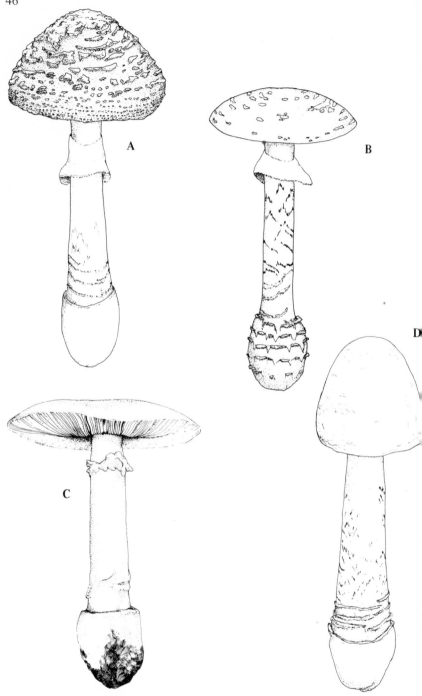

PL. 16. **Types of Volvas A.**, **B.** scaly, **C.** circumsessile, **D.** concentric ringed (zoned).

L. 17. **Sporocarp Attachment & Shape A.** pileate & sessile — ungulate, **B.** pileate & sessile, . substipitate due to a pseudostipe, **D.** imbricate.

termed **stipitate**. However, other attachments are seen. Sometimes a flap of tissue (but not the pileus) that is not distinctly a stalk serves for attachment. This structure is called a **pseudostipe**, and the condition is described as **substipitate**. If the attachment is directly to the pileus with no stipe or pseudostipe, the mushroom is referred to as **sessile** (Plate 17C).

Sessile fruiting bodies vary in the degree to which the pileus is attached. It is called **pileate and sessile** if it is attached in one place in such a way that the

Pileate and sessile (Pl. 17A,B)	pileus is still definitely observable. If part of the fruiting body is closely appressed to the substrate except for the margin which flares out to form the
Effuso-reflexed (Fig. 7A)	pileus, it is called **effuso-reflexed**. If the entire fruiting body looks like a horse's hoof, it is called
Imbricate (Pl. 17D)	**ungulate**. And, if the complete fruiting body is closely appressed to the substrate, it is called
Resupinate (Fig. 7B)	**resupinate**. At times, fruiting bodies overlap one another, and this condition is called **imbricate**.

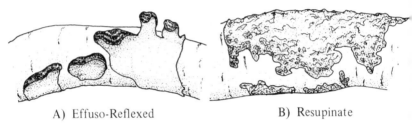

A) Effuso-Reflexed   B) Resupinate

FIGURE 7: Types of Fruiting Body Attachment

H. SPORE COLOR

Probably the single most important feature to learn about mushrooms is the color of the basidiospores *en masse*. The best way to determine this is to make a *spore print*. Spore prints can be taken of agarics, boletes, chantrelles, polypores, teeth fungi and coral fungi; but not of puff balls and their allies such as stink horns, earth stars, etc.

To make a spore print, select a fresh but mature fruiting body and cut off the stipe at the apex. Place the cap flat on a piece of white paper or cardboard with the spore-bearing surface (gills, pores, etc.) down. Then cover the cap and paper entirely in wax paper or in a jar or retain in a tin to eliminate air currents. If the fruiting body is in the right condition, you should have a print within 30 or 60 minutes. Spore prints can be begun in the field immediately after collecting, or one can wait and do it later at home or in the laboratory.

Sometimes the spore print will not work. When this happens, there are still ways to estimate the color of spores. One trick is to look in places where spores might naturally be deposited, such as along the stipe of the same mushroom. If your mushrooms have been piled on top of one another in your collecting basket, or growing that way naturally, look at the top of the cap directly below

e mushroom in question. In both of these cases, however, take care not to
ɔnfuse color of the fruiting body itself with spore color. Futhermore realize
aat damp spores are often more strongly colored than those which are dry.
ften, masses of spores can be seen on the substrate, directly beneath the
ushroom in its natural habitat. If no evidence of masses of liberated spores can
ɛ found, examine the color of the gills of a mature specimen. Often, especially
those mushrooms with white or pallid colored gills, the color of the mature
lls reflects the color of the spores. CAUTION! This last shortcut is only
curate about two-thirds of the time. There are many examples of mushrooms
ıving white spores and brown, black, gray, lilac, or pink gills. Consequently,
ıe should rely on this method only after all other alternatives have been tried.
you are planning to eat the mushroom, and there is any doubt in your mind
ɔout the spore color, throw the specimens away!

The color of the spores in mass can be put into the following five general
ıtegories.

1) Spores bright or light colored − includes white, pale cream to cream
ɔlored, pale to bright yellow (greenish in one case).

2) Spores salmon to pink colored − more appropriately called flesh or flesh-
ɔwn colored.

3) Spores various shades of yellow brown or brown − clay colored, clay-
ɔwn, yellow-brown, cinnamon-brown, earth color, rust color, or rusty-brown.

4) Spores purple brown to chocolate brown.

5) Spores smoke color to dark gray brown to black.

GUIDELINES FOR SAFE MUSHROOM COLLECTING
(Adapted from Spore Prints[1])

Mushroom collecting has been called the most dangerous of outdoor sports.
is will not be true if we play by the rules.

A. Know precisely and positively what you're after when collecting for the
ɔle.

B. Collect only one species at a time. In case you do collect more than one
ɛcies, keep each kind and each collection separate. I find it best to place each
llection in a separate wax container − either waxed sandwich bags (use
ıterials similar to waxtex, NOT baggies or their equivalent because they cause
reased temperature and humidity that hastens the spoiling process) or wax
ɔer. *Never mix more than one species in a single wax container. Never just*
ow all kinds of mushrooms in the same basket.

C. Use a flat, rigid container such as a cardboard box or a wicker basket for a
lecting container. Make sure it has good, securely attached handles. A student
mine, Robert Smith, prepared a box as follows: He punched holes in opposite
ners of a cardboard box, through which he threaded a solid rope. The area
ere the rope was to be held was taped for a better grip. He then sprayed the

his section is a modified version of an article that first appeared in *The Spore Prints* the
ɯsletter of the Puget Sound Mycological Society which in turn came from a pamphlet
led May is Morel Month by Ingrid Bartelli.

box, inside and out, with a good water repellant, and finally waxed the bo
using melted paraffin, which he applied with a paint brush. After leaving to dry
overnight, he was able to use the box, rain or shine, for most of one collectin
season. Such a rigid container prevents undue crushing of the mushrooms an
does not spill easily.

D. Only young and fresh specimens are suitable for food. After a mushroom
matures and begins to deteriorate, its edible qualities likewise deteriorate.

E. Keep your collections as clean as possible. Pick the entire fruiting body s
you are positive it's the right kind. Clean off any dirt before placing in the wa
container, but *be careful* not to remove the volva, scales, or any othe
identifying characteristics.

F. Have a trimming or cutting knife, preferably in a sheath. Unless you wan
to keep knife manufacturers in business, I find it a necessity to drill a hole in th
handle and attach it with a chain or rope to the basket.

G. Have a pencil and notebook or 3x5 cards in case you wish to make note
or leave any notes (should you get lost). Note the substrate, tree(s) associate
with the mushroom, and the elevation.

H. Have a compass available and note the direction of your car.

I. Keep collected specimens in as good shape and as well aired as is possib
until you get home.

J. When home, put your mushrooms in a cool, dry, shaded place, preferabl
a refrigerator, or under the house, until you are ready to identify them. If yo
have collected the fungi in wet weather, you may want to change the wet wa
containers for dry ones.

K. Clean, process and cook your mushrooms as soon as possible after you ge
home. Most mushrooms deteriorate very rapidly after they are picked. To clean
split the cap lengthwise to check for spoilage or insect infestation.

L. Get yourself a good manual on fungal toxins. The Puget Sound Myco
logical Society has one available for $1.50, entitled *Mushroom Toxins*.

M. The first time you eat a mushroom, *eat sparingly*! You'll want to observ
your reaction to it. Always save a few fresh specimens for identification in cas
you become ill.

N. And what if you should make a mistake? If you should eat a poisonou
mushroom, empty your stomach and call a doctor. Then keep your manual o
mushroom toxins handy for consultation.

II. PART TWO

A. STATURE TYPES OF FRUITING BODIES

If you have followed the organization of this book thus far you *now* should have a firm foundation in understanding the various macroscopic features of mushrooms. You should be able to go out into the field, collect various mushrooms and properly describe the features of the pileus, gills, and stipe.

But, up until now we have discussed the features of the fruiting body as though they were independent of each other. However, *certain families of features are seen to occur together in recognizable combinations*. These combinations were first recognized by Elias Fries, the grand master of agaricologists, and have been used extensively by the English agaricologists like Rea and Massee. Combinations are extremely useful for many reasons. It forces the student to study the *whole* fruiting body and to correlate series of features rather than one or two at a time and more importantly to study over and over again the macroscopic features of the mushrooms. Additionally, one can identify fleshy fungi at least to genus with some degree of certainty.

CAUTION. Mushrooms vary a great deal with age and environmental conditions. Therefore, do not expect to identify all mushrooms to genus using the following diagrammatic charts. Also, expect variation and when in doubt, use the dichotomous key that follows.

Stature Types are based on the following important features.

1. Presence or absence of an annulus.
2. Presence or absence of a volva.
3. Consistency of stipe.
4. Attachment of stipe.
5. Attachment of gills.
6. Shape of pileus.
7. Type of pileal margin.

Note: The classification used in the following pages follows more or less that found in C. H. Kauffman's *Agaricaceae of Michigan* with some notable exceptions. No attempt has been made to incorporate the new or less widely accepted mushroom names because these are constantly changing. The same classification system with some exceptions is used in the reference books cited in the back of this book.

Thirteen stature types are presented and the important features to notice are found at the top of the charts as well as additional features listed to the right or left of the diagram which is typical of that particular stature type. I have tried to use a name of a common genus of mushrooms to assist you in understanding the stature types. The first twelve have a centrally attached stipe.

1. Types with Free or Finely Adnexed Gills

The first set of types are similar in that each one has either free gills or finely adnexed gills which appear as if they are free to the naked eye and a centrally attached stipe. Each stature type with this type of gill and stipe attachment varies from each other on the presence and/or absence of a volva and/or an annulus (not a ***cortina***). Please note that some features are not involved in these stature types — such as the consistence of the stipe, shape of the pileus or the type of pileal margin. The following possibilities exist:

Choices	1	2	3	4
annulus	present	absent	present	absent
volva	present	present	absent	absent

Choice #1 is called **Amanitoid**, after the genus *Amanita* which typifies this stature type, and which is the only genus of mushrooms found in North America with free to finely adnexed gills and the presence of both an annulus and a volva.

Choice #2 is called **Vaginatoid** after the old genus *Vaginata* which is synonymous with *Amanitopsis*. The latter is now considered synonymous with *Amanita*. All mushrooms with free or finely adnexed gills and the presence of a volva are considered to have a Vaginatoid Stature.

Choice #3 represents those mushrooms with an annulus but not a volva and do have a centrally attached stipe and free or finely adnexed gills. This stature type is called **Lepiotoid** after the genus *Lepiota* which typifies it.

The last choice, #4, is typical of those mushrooms with no annulus nor volva but ***with*** free gills. Such a stature type is called **Pluteotoid** and is typified by the genus *Pluteus*.

These are summarized in Plate 18.

FIGURE 8: Zoned Volva of *Amanita muscaria*

PLATE 18

STATURE TYPES WITH FREE OR FINELY ATTACHED GILLS

Amanitoid

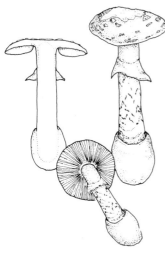

Annulus: present
Volva: present

Vaginatoid

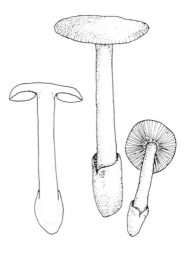

Annulus: Absent
Volva: Present

Lepiotoid

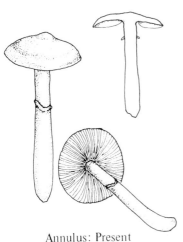

Annulus: Present
Volva: Absent

Pluteotoid

Annulus: Absent
Volva: Absent

2. Types with Attached Gills and a Central, Fleshy-Fibrou Stipe

The stature types diagrammed on the opposite page (Plate 19) have th following features in common:

1) the gills are attached to the stipe.
2) the stipe is either fleshy fibrous or chalky in consistency.
3) the stipe is centrally attached or possibly very slightly excentric.
4) a volva is absent.

The features which vary are the presence or absence of an annulus and th specific kind of gill attachment. Please note that some features are not used i these stature types — namely, the type of pileal margin and the pileal shape.

The **Armillarioid** type is the only one with an annulus; the gill attachmer varies within the various genera. The type is named after *Armillaria* which is th most typical genus.

The three remaining types differ from each other by the type of gi attachment. Those with sinuate (or notched) gills are called **Tricholomatoi** based on the genus *Tricholoma*; those with adnate, adnexed or emarginate gil are called **Naucorioid** after *Naucoria*; and those with any type of decurrent gi attachment are called **Clitocyboid** after the genus *Clitocybe*.

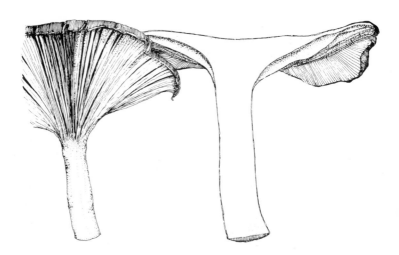

FIGURE 9: Decurrent gills of *Clitocybe avellaneialba*

PLATE 19

STATURE TYPES WITH ATTACHED GILLS
AND A FLESHY-FIBROUS STIPE

Tricholomatoid

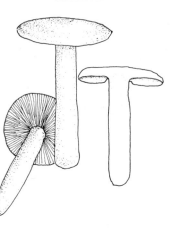

Gill Attachment: Sinuate or Notched
Annulus: Absent

Armillarioid

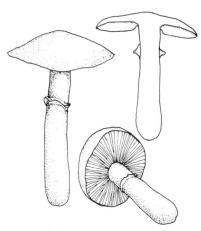

Gill Attachment: Variable
Annulus: Present

Clitocyboid

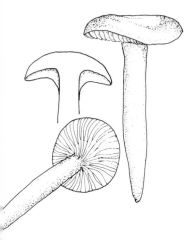

Gill Attachment: Decurrent, Arcuate-
                Decurrent
                or Subdecurrent
Annulus: Absent

Naucorioid

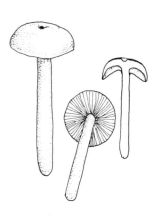

Gill Attachment: Adnate,
                Adnexed or Emarginate
Annulus: Absent

3. Types with Attached Gills and a Central, Cartilaginous Stipe

These stature types as seen from the diagrams to the right (Plate 20) are groupings of those rather small (in most instances), fragile mushrooms with cartilaginous, centrally attached stipes and attached gills. In these hed stipes and attached gills. In these examples, the only feature not emphasized is the volva which is absent in almost all examples.

The types are separated on variations in pileal shape, pileal margin, gill attachment and the presence or absence of an annulus. Four types can be observed: **Mycenoid** with *Mycena* being the typical genus, **Collybioid** based on *Collybia*, **Omphalinoid** based on *Omphalina* and **Anellarioid** with *Anellaria* the most typical. They differ as follows:

Type	Pileal Shape	Pileal Margin When Young	Gill Attachment	Annulus
Mycenoid	Conic to Campanulate	Decurved or straight to the stem	Variable but not decurrent	Usually absent
Collybioid	Convex to Parabolic	Incurved to Decurved	Variable but not decurrent	Usually absent
Omphalinoid	Broadly Convex to Plane	Variable	Decurrent Subdecurrent Arcuate-decurrent	Absent
Anellarioid	Variable	Variable	Variable	Present

FIGURE 10: Double Annulus of *Agaricus* sp.

PLATE 20

STATURE TYPES WITH ATTACHED GILLS
AND A CARTILAGINOUS STIPE

Mycenoid

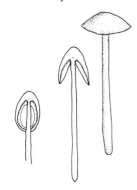

Pileus: Conic to Campanulate
Pileal Margin: Decurved at first
Gill Attachment: Variable but not
decurrent
Annulus: Absent
Volva: Absent

Collybioid

Pileus: Convex
Pileal Margin: Incurved to Inrolled at first
Gill Attachment: Variable but not decurrent
Annulus: Absent
Volva: Absent

Omphaloid

Pileus: Broadly Convex to Plane and at times
Umbilicate
Pileal Margin: Variable
Gill Attachment: Decurrent to Subdecurrent
Annulus: Absent
Volva: Absent

Anellarioid

Pileus: Variable
Pileal Margin: Variable
Gill Attachment: Variable
Annulus: Present
Volva: Absent

4. Type with an Excentric or Lateral Attached Stipe, Or The Stipe is Absent

The last stature type, **Pleurotoid**, is diagrammed to the right. (Plate 21) It encompasses all those mushrooms with distinctly laterally attached or distinctly excentric stipes such as most species of *Pleurotus* which is the genus after which the stature type was named. This stature type is admittedly articifical since the genera included are classified in several, different families.

FIGURE 11: Free Gills of *Pluteus cervinus*

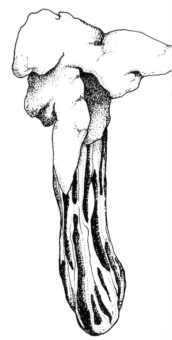

FIGURE 12: Lacunose Stipe of the Ascomycete, *Helvella lacunosa*

PLATE 21

STATURE TYPES WITH AN EXCENTRIC
OR LATERALLY ATTACHED STIPE
OR WITHOUT A STIPE

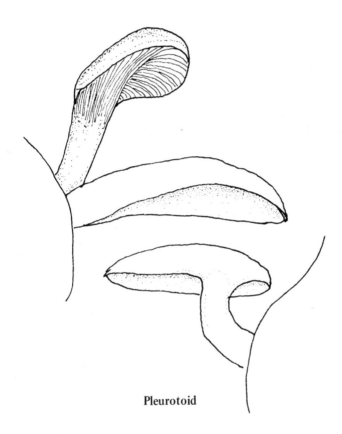

Pleurotoid

III. PART THREE

The following pages organize the various genera of mushrooms which can easily be identified on macroscopic features into their respective stature types. As can be seen from the charts, the genera within a common stature type differ only in spore color and have a whole series of features in common. Elias Fries the grand master of agaricology, recognized this when organizing the mushrooms into his classification schemes. Similar sounding names were used, I surmise, to emphasize the fact that these mushrooms had many features in common and differed from each other mainly in spore color – e.g. *Tricholoma, Hebeloma, Entoloma*, and *Hypholoma* all have a tricholomatoid habit and differ respectively by having white, pink, brown, and purple brown spores. Other examples of similar sounding names, the same stature type, but having different spore color are *Pleurotus, Claudopus, Crepidotus* all with Pleurotoid habit and *Armillaria* and *Stropharia* with an Armillarioid habit.

To use these charts, scrutinize the mushroom you desire identified and identify its stature type. These are located in the left vertical column of the chart. **Then**, identify the spore color and locate the proper choice from the five possibilities on the top of the chart. Come down the vertical column of the appropriate spore color until it meets the chosen stature type. This will place you within one square within which are either one genus name or more than one. If just one name – you will find page reference to three reference books to assist in identifying the species as follows:

Miller – *Mushrooms of North America* . . . . .M
Stuntz & McKenny – *The Savory Wild Mushroom* . . . . . . .S-M
Smith – *Mushroom Hunters Field Guide* . . . . .S

If more than one genus name appears, you will find a number which refers you to the key line number in the key found beginning on page 00. You can either key the mushroom to genus from that point or attempt to identify the mushroom to genus by referring to the respective genera found in the indices of the reference books.

The use of stature types to identify mushrooms to genus is **by no means infallible**. Numerous problems arise due to environmental variations such as the weather is too dry or due to changes of the fruiting body with time such as the annulus falling off of *Coprinus comatus* or the partial veil disappearing in *Stropharia ambigua* or the difficulty in determining the type of pileal margin, or the presence of an annulus in *Tricholoma cingulatum* – or, or, or. But you can use stature types to identify many mushrooms to genus – review the charts and you will see that 26 spaces out of 46 have only a single genus. The usefulness of stature types is basically twofold; it narrows down the possible choices you have to make to identify the mushroom and, more important in my opinion, it makes you carefully look at your mushrooms and make some critical evaluations of many of the important macroscopic features. But remember – the cardinal rule in all identification procedures – if you absolutely can't identify a feature with 100% certainty either consult a specialist who can or **throw the mushroom away**.

A. GENERA WITH FREE OR FINELY ADNEXED GILLS

Spore Color / Type	WHITE	PINK	BROWN	PURPLE-BROWN	BLACK
Amanitoid	*Armillaria* #26 *Amanita* #26			*Clarkeinda* (rare, tropical, Asia)	
Vaginatoid	*Amanita* S-170 M-25 SM-26	*Volvariella* M-105 SM-110		*Agaricus* S-189 M-126 SM-136	*Coprinus* S-222 M-113 SM-154
Lepiotoid	*Lepiota* #32 *Amanita* #32	*Chamaeota*		*Agaricus* S-189 M-126 SM-136	*Coprinus* S-222 M-113 SM-154
Pluteotoid	*Hygrophorus* #47 *Lepiota* #47 *Amanita* #47	*Pluteus* S-200 M-105 SM-112	*Pluteolus*	*Agaricus* S-189 M-126 SM-136	*Coprinus* S-222 M-113 SM-154

B. GENERA WITH ATTACHED GILLS AND A FLESHY-FIBROUS STIPE

Spore Color / Type	WHITE TO CREAM TO YELLOW	PINK	BROWN	PURPLE-BROWN	BLACK
Tricholomatoid	Tricholoma #86 Russula (stipe chalky) #86 Hygrophorus (stipe not chalky) #86	Entoloma #89 Tricholoma #89	Naucoria #91 Hebeloma #91 Inocybe #91 Cortinarius #91 Pholiota (Flammula) #91 Paxillus #91	Hypholoma M-119	
Naucorioid	Clitocybe #19 Russula #19 (chalky) Lactarius #86 Hygrophorus #86 Laccaria #86 (not chalky)	Entoloma M-107 SM-114	Naucoria #91 Hebeloma #91 Inocybe #91 Cortinarius #91 Pholiota (Flammula) #91		
Clitocyboid	Russula #19 Lactarius #19 (chalky) Hygrophorus #65 Clitocybe #65 (not chalky)	Clitopilus M-107	Paxillus #69 Pholiota (Flammula) #69 Inocybe #69		Gomphidius S-227 M-109 SM-151
Armillarioid	Armillaria #26 & 29 Amanita #26 & 29 Lentinus #29		Flammula #36 Hebeloma #36 Pholiota #36	Stropharia #44 Hypholoma #44	Gomphidius S-227 M-109 SM-151

C. GENERA WITH ATTACHED GILLS AND A CARTILAGINOUS STIPE

Spore Color / Type	WHITE – YELLOW	PINK	BROWN	PURPLE-BROWN	BLACK
Mycenoid	*Mycena* #73 *Marasmius* #73	*Nolanea*	*Galerina* #78 *Bolbitius* #78 *Naucoria* #78	*Psilocybe* #82 *Psathyrella* #82 *Panaeolus* #82	*Coprinus* #84 *Panaeolus* #84 *Psathyrella* #84
Collybioid	*Collybia* #73 *Marasmius* #73	*Leptonia* #76 *Nolanea* #76	*Bolbitius* #78 *Naucoria* #78	*Psilocybe* M-122 SM-210	*Coprinus* S-122 M-113 SM-154
Omphaloid	*Marasmius* #62 *Omphalina* #62	*Leptonia*	*Tubaria*	*Psilocybe* M-122 SM-210	
Anellarioid			*Galerina* S-215 M-141 SM-134	*Psilocybe* M-122 SM-210	*Psathyrella* #84 *Panaeolus (Anellaria)* #84 *Coprinus* #84

64

D. GENERA WITH AN ECENTRICALLY OR LATERAL ATTACHED STIPE OR WITHOUT A STIPE

Spore Color / Type	WHITE	PINK	BROWN	PURPLE-BROWN	BLACK
Pleurotoid	Schizophyllum #12 Pleurotus #12 Panus #12 Lentinus #12 Plicatura #12 Lenzites #12	Claudopus	Crepidotus #11 Paxillus #11		

IV. PART FOUR

. KEY TO IDENTIFY MUSHROOMS TO GENUS USING ONLY MACROSCOPIC FEATURES (*)

In this key, only characteristics of the mushrooms that can be seen with the aided eye (or at most with a handlens) are used. Bear in mind that it is next to possible to construct, with such a basis, a key that will lead unerringly to the rrect genus, and be prepared to explore the alternative key leads, if the ones u have chosen seem to be getting you nowhere.

The key herein presented is called a dichotomous key since it presents you th *two* choices at each step. To use the key, pretend the two choices, each th the same number, are actually two separate questions which can be swered with a yes or no answer. For example, choice #1 could be written . . ." the sporocarp (= fruiting body) I have, attached directly to the fruiting bodies other mushrooms? *or* is it not growing on other mushrooms?" You must have e yes answer and one no answer; whichever choice is yes you are to follow a tted line and another number is given. This number is the choice on the key. r example, if you answered yes to Sporocarp not growing on other shrooms, you are referred to choice 5. Again two choices are present – if you swer yes to the second choice you are referred to choice #8. Choice 8 asks u if the sporocarp has a pleurotoid habit or not. If it does you are referred to oice 9. If your pleurotoid fungus has pink spores, you answer yes to the first the two choices and you've identified the mushroom as a *Claudopus* species. If you answer no to both choices, you've made an error and must backtrack the previous choice until you reach a point where you were not 100% sure of ur decision. You've most probably made an error at this point and should try e alternative choice. To assist you in backtracking, notice that some of the key oices have another number in parentheses immediately following it. This is the mber which led you to your choice, for example to get to key choice #8 you d to say yes to one of the two choices in key choice #5.

Once you've identified the mushroom to genus you will find letters and mbers following it which will not only help you verify your identification, but ll also help you make a species identification. The numbers refer to pages in erence books, the letters identify the reference books as follows:

    M   = Miller, Mushrooms of North America
    K   = Kauffman, Agaricaceae of Michigan
    SM = Stuntz & McKenny, The Savory Wild Mushroom
    S   = Smith, Mushroom Hunter's Field Guide

But remember, if you aren't 100% positive *either consult a specialist or throw e mushroom away*.

Good Luck & Good Hunting.

onstructed mostly by Dr. Daniel E. Stuntz, University of Washington.

66

1. Sporocarp attached directly to the sporocarps of other
mushrooms (e.g., parasitic on mushrooms) 2

1. Sporocarp not growing on other mushrooms 5

    2. Volva present; gills free; spores pink . . . . *Volvariella* (K526,
SM110, M87)

    2. Volva lacking; attachment of gills varies; spores
white or purple-brown 3

3. Spores purple-brown; stipe with a floccose white
annulus . . . . *Stropharia* (K246
M119, SM146, S216

3. Spores white; stipe lacking an annulus .4

    4. Pileus 1 cm. or more broad; stipe 3 mm or more thick,
fleshy or pulpy, not arising from a sclerotium; gills
often thick and vein-like, or more or less suppressed;
pileal context becoming transformed into a powdery
mass of chlamydospores . . . . *Asterophora* (K3
M62

    4. Pileus less than 1 cm. in diam.; stipe 1-2 mm thick,
arising from a small sclerotium that resembles a
grain of wheat; gills normal, well developed; pileal
context not becoming transformed into chlamydospores . . . . . *Collyb*
(K749, S135, M89, SM105

5. (1) Instead of normal, blade-like gills, the under
surface of the pileus bears folds or wrinkles with
blunt, rounded edges, or bears a network of thick,
obtuse veins 6

5. Under surface of pileus with normal, blade-like gills 8

    6. Sporocarps terrestrial, often funnel-shaped or
trumpet-shaped, or with a stem and funnel-like,
flaring pileus . . . . *Cantharellus* &
Gomphus (K32, M149
SM22, S122

    6. Sporocarps lignicolous, sometimes stipitate, but
the pileus not trumpet-shaped or funnel-shaped 7

7. Pileus sessile, laterally attached, shelving, or
shell-shaped . . . .*Plicatura* (K4

7. Pileus stipitate . . . . *Marasmius* (K57, M8
SM109, S135, 15

8. (5) Pileus sessile; laterally attached and shelving, or attached by a short lateral tubercle or "pseudo-stipe", or basally attached and funnel-shaped or spatulate (Pleurotoid habit) 9

8. Pileus with a definite stipe, that may be central, eccentric, or (rarely) even lateral 17

9. Spores pink or salmon-color or brownish pink ...... *Claudopus* (K590, all others see *Rhodophyllus* M109, SM114, S201)

9. Spores not pink, salmon-color, or brownish pink 10

10. Spores some shade of brown or brownish ochre 11

10. Spores white to *pale* yellowish or cream color, or (rarely) *pale* dingy lilac 12

1. The whole hymenophore readily peeling away from the pileus as a unit; gills strongly intervenose, often almost poroid, near the point of attachment .... *Paxillus* (K284, M130, SM128, S204)

1. Hymenophore not separable as a unit from the pileus (but *individual gills* may break off readily); gills not strongly intervenose at the point of attachment .... *Crepidotus* (K516, M134)

12. (10) Gills split longitudinally along their edges, and rolled back laterally, hence appearing like two parallel, radially oriented tubes .... *Schizophyllum* (K42, M67)

12. Gills not split along their edges and rolled back laterally 13

3. Gills narrow, strongly crisped and sinuous; pileus thin, membranous, tough and pliable (when moist) .... *Plicatura* (K41)

3. Gills narrow or broad, but not strongly crisped or sinuous; pileal thickness varies, but if thin enough to be membranous, it is also soft and fleshy 14

14. Pileus very tough and corky; gills tough and leathery .... *Lenzites* (not included by K; M183)

14. Pileus varying in consistency from soft and pulpy to pliable or leathery, but not corky; gills not tough and leathery 15

68

15. Edge of gills serrated .... *Lentinus* (K49, M64, S134)

15. Edge of gills entire (even) 16

    16. Pileus tough and pliable or fibrous .... *Panus* (K43,M74)

    16. Pileus soft and pulpy or fleshy .... *Pleurotus* (K656, M69, SM79, S134)

17. (8) Gills deliquescent (in mature sporocarps) 18
17. Gills not deliquescent 19

    18. Spores black .... *Coprinus* (K206, M113, SM156, S222)

    18. Spores rusty brown .... *Bolbitius* (K502, M132)

19. (17) Stipe breaking like soft chalk, without any trace of fibrous context 20

19. Stipe when broken or split lengthwise showing evidence of fibrous context 21

    20. Sporocarp exuding a watery or milky or colored juice where cut .... *Lactarius* (K83 M46, SM94, S231)

    20. Sporocarp not exuding a juice where cut .... *Russula* (K118, M56, SM82, S249)

21. (19) Volva present 22

21. Volva not present 27

    22. Gills free 23

    22. Gills attached 26

23. Spores purple-brown (*mature* gills dark brownish purple or chocolate color) .... *Agaricu* (=*Psalliota*) (K232 M126, SM136, S189)

23. Spores pink or white (mature gills never purplish brown or chocolate color) 24

    24. Spores pink (*mature* gills definitely pink or dingy salmon color) .... *Volvariell* (=*Volvaria*) (K526 SM110, M87)

    24. Spores white to *pallid* yellowish (mature gills not pink or salmon color) 25

25. Annulus present .... *Amanita* (K593, M25, SM26, S170)

25. Annulus lacking .... *Vaginata* (=*Amanitopsis*) (now put in *Amanita*) (K621)

   26. (22) Volva sheathing the entire lower half or two thirds of the stipe, and flaring outwards at its upper edge .. *Armillaria* (K647, M74, SM43, S134)

   26. Volva truly basal, not sheathing the lower part of the stipe (but it may sheath the **bulb** at the base of the stipe) .... *Amanita* (K593, M25, SM26, S170)

27. (21) Annulus present 28

27. Annulus lacking 45

   28. Spores either white to pallid yellowish or pale cream color, or pink to dingy salmon-pink 29

   28. Spores some shade of brown, purple-brown, or black 35

29. Edge of the gills serrated; pileal context and stipe tough and pliable .... *Lentinus* (K49, M64, S134)

29. Edge of the gills entire; pileal context and stipe soft, pulpy, or fleshy-fibrous 30

   30. Gills free 31

   30. Gills attached 34

31. Spores pink or dingy salmon-pink .... *Chamaeota* (K533)

31. Spores white to pallid yellowish or pale cream color 32

   32. Pileal surface truly viscid .... *Lepiota* (K625, M34, SM40, S170)

   32. Pileal surface not truly viscid (it may be **lubricous** in fresh, moist plants) 33

33. Pileal surface bearing remnants of the universal veil, in the form of felty or friable warts or patches, on a smooth, glabrous surface .... *Amanita* (K593, M25, SM26, S170)

33. Pileal surface not with warts or patches of universal veil; it is, however, often scaly .... *Lepiota* (K625, M34, SM40, S186)

34. (30) Gills only slightly attached, *and* stipe with
a conspicuous bulbous base .... *Amanita* (K593, M25
SM26, S170

34. Gills definitely attached; stipe with or without
a bulbous base (usually if the base is bulbous, the
gills are more or less decurrent) .... *Armillaria* (K64
M74, SM43, S134

35. (28) Spores orange-brown, bright rusty brown, dull
rusty brown, cinnamon-brown, dull earthy brown, or
umbre 36

35. Spores purple-brown, dusky purple, or black 40

36. Sporocarps lignicolous 37

36. Sporocarps terrestrial 38

37. Annulus only slightly developed, consisting of an
inconspicuous band of fibrils; stipe not scaly .... *Flammula* (K483, M140

37. Annulus well developed and conspicuous (often membranous,
or even felty), or stipe definitely scaly, or both .... *Pholio.*
(K289, M137, SM118, S20°

38. (36) Pileus viscid 39

38. Pileus not viscid .... *Pholiota* (see abov

39. Pileus scaly; or if it is glabrous, then the stipe is
conspicuously peronate below the annulus with floccose
material .... *Pholiota* (see abov

39. Pileus glabrous, *and* stipe more or less fibrillose below
the annulus, but not peronate with floccose material
(in *Hebeloma*) or annulate (in *Agrocybe, Rozites*) ...... *Hebeloma* (K46
M144, SM128
Agrocybe (M13°
Rozites (M140, SM11:
S21°

40. (35) Gills free .... *Agaricus* (=Psalliot
(K232, M126, SM13
S18°

40. Gills attached 41

41. Annulus dry; membranous, floccose, or fibrillose; pileus
may or may not be viscid, but the stipe is not viscid below
the annulus 43

41. Annulus viscid, collapsing as a viscous band upon the
stipe; pileus and stipe (below the annulus) also viscid 42

42. Gills strongly decurrent, rather thick and
subdistant; spores black .... *Gomphidius* (K 169,
M 109, SM 151, S 227)

42. Gills adnexed to squarely adnate or slightly
uncinate, but not truly decurrent, not thick, not subdistant; spores blackish purple or purple-brown .... *Stropharia* (K 246,
M 119, SM 146, S 216)

3. (41) Pileus bell-shaped or parabolic, not expanding;
gills mottled by the maturation of the spores in
distinct patches; spores black .... *Panaeolus* (K 228,
M 117, SM 158)

3. Pileus expanding and becoming campanulate to convex or
plane; gills uniformly colored; spores purple-brown
or blackish purple 44

44. Annulus thin and poorly developed, because most of the
velar material adheres to the margin of the pileus;
sporocarps lignicolous .... *Hypholoma* (K 254,
M 119)

44. Annulus membranous and usually well developed, if
velar material adheres to the margin of the pileus,
sporocarps terrestrial .... *Stropharia* (K 246,
M 119, SM 146, S 216)

5. (27) Gills free 46

5. Gills attached 52

46. Spores white to pale yellowish or cream color 47

46. Spores pink, brown, purple-brown, or black 49

7. Pileus viscid; gills thick, subdistant, and waxy-looking ...... *Hygrophorus*
(K 172, M 38, SM 69, S 229)

7. Pileus not viscid; gills not thick and waxy-looking 48

48. Large, fleshy sporocarps; pileus 5 cm or more in
diameter, stipe more than 5 mm thick .... *Amanita* (K 593
M 25, SM 216, S 170)

48. Medium-sized or small, slender sporocarps; pileus usually
less than 5 cm in diameter, stipe 1-5 mm thick ... *Lepiota* (K 625, M 34,
SM 40, S 186)

9. (46) Spores pink (mature gills pink or rose-salmon) . *Pluteus* (K 535, M 105,
SM 112, S 200)

9. Spores brown or purple-brown or black 50

50. Spores bright rusty brown or orange-brown; pileus
viscid .... *Pluteolus* (K 50

50. Spores purple-brown or chocolate brown or black 51

51. Pileus fleshy (context at least 2-3 mm thick at the center);
stipe fleshy-fibrous; spores purple-brown or chocolate
color .... *Agaricus* (= *Psalliot*
(K 232, M 126, SM 13
S 18

51. Pileus membranous (context usually 1 mm or less thick at
the center); stipe fragile; spores black .... *Coprinus* (K 2
M 113, SM 156, S 22

    52. Flesh of mature, fresh pilei soft and pulpy to soft-
    to leathery, or even corky (reviving when moistened
    after having been dried); spores white to pale
    yellowish 53

    52. Flesh of mature, fresh pilei soft and pulpy to soft-
    fibrous, or very fragile (not reviving when moistened
    after having been dried); spores white, pink, brown,
    purple-brown, or black 55

53. Edge of gills serrated .... *Lentinus* (K 49, M (
S 13

53. Edge of gills entire 54

    54. Stipe slender, usually 1-3 mm thick, or at least less
    than 5 mm in diameter, often corneous or very tough-
    elastic; pileal context usually membranous and pliable ..... *Marasm*
    (K 57, M 80, SM 109, S 135, 15

    54. Stipe stouter than in the above, 5 mm or more thick;
    pileal context thick, usually more or less rigid, or
    at least very firm .... *Panus* (K 43, M (

55. (52) Stipe definitely and consistently eccentric, sometimes almost lateral 56

55. Stipe central, or nearly so 59

    56. Spores white to pale yellowish or cream color,
    or pallid lilac .... *Pleurotus* (see a
    some species of *Pan*
    (K 656, M 69, SM
    S 1

    56. Spores pink or brownish salmon, or some shade of
    ochre or brown 57

⁷. Spores yellowish brown, or ochraceous ....*Paxillus* (K284, M130
SM128, S204)

⁷. Spores pink or dingy salmon-color 58

   58. Gills strongly decurrent .... *Clitopilus* (K562,
M107)

   58. Gills adnexed to adnate, not decurrent ....*Entoloma* (K545)
(see *Rhodophyllus*
M109, SM114, S201)

⁹. (55) Gills definitely decurrent, or at least broadly
adnate-subdecurrent 60

⁹. Gills variously attached, but neither adnate-subdecurrent
nor decurrent 71

   60. Stipe slender, about 1-3 mm in diameter, always less than
5 mm thick, often fibrous-pliant, or fragile, or brittle;
pileal flesh thin, often membranous 61

   60. Stipe stouter than the above, 5 mm or more thick,
fleshy-fibrous and soft, or pulpy, or with a firm
cartilaginous "rind" and soft interior; pileal
flesh ordinarily at least 3-5 mm thick at the center,
rarely thin enough to be called membranous 65,

⒈ Spores white to pale yellowish or pallid cream color 62

⒈ Spores pink, or dingy salmon-color, or some shade of
yellow-brown or umber, or purple-brown 63

   62. Stipe corneous and rigid, or tough-elastic ...... *Marasmius* (K57, M80,
SM109, S135,155)

   62. Stipe soft and fleshy, often brittly or fragile . *Omphalina* (= *Omphalia*)
(K812, M83)

⒊ (61) Spores pink (mature lamellae becoming pink) .... *Leptonia* (see
Rhodophyllus M109,
SM114, S201)

⒊ Spores some shade of brown, or purple-brown 64

   64. Spores purple-brown, or brownish *red*, or chocolate-
color with a purplish cast .... *Psilocybe* (K272,
M122, SM210)

   64. Spores rusty brown or yellowish brown ....*Tubaria* (not recognized by Kauffman)

⒌ (60) Spores white to pale cream color 66

⒌ Spores pink, dingy salmon-color, brownish salmon,
yellow-brown, ochraceous, rusty brown, umber, or black 67

66. Gills thick, subdistant, and waxy-looking .... *Hygrophorus* (K17
M38, SM69, S229

66. Gills thin, usually at least close, sometimes
crowded, and not waxy-appearing ....*Clitocybe* (K715, M8
SM58, S135

67. (65) Spores pink, dingy salmon-pink, or brownish salmon ...... *Clitopilu*
(K562, M107

67. Spores ochraceous to rusty brown, or umber, or black 68

68. Spores rusty brown, umber, or cinnamon-brown 69

68. Spores black .... *Gomphidius* (K16
M109, SM151, S22

69. The entire hymenophore peeling away as a unit from the
pileal flesh; either the stipe is covered with dark
brown to black velvety hairs, or the gills quickly stain
reddish brown where bruised .... *Paxillus* (K28
M130, SM128, S20

69. Hymenophore not separating readily as a unit from the
pileal flesh (though *individual gills* can be broken off
readily); stipe neither velvety, nor gills bruising
reddish-brown 70

70. Lignicolous, or if terrestrial, then also the pileus
is viscid .... *Flammula* (K483, M14
70. Terrestrial, *and* the pileus not viscid .... *Inocybe* (K442, M14
SM13

71. (59) Stipe slender, about 1-3 mm in diameter, always
less than 5 mm thick, often fibrous-pliant, or brittle, or
fragile; pileal flesh thin, often membranous 72

71. Stipe stouter than the above, 5 mm or more thick, fleshy-
fibrous and soft, or pulpy, or with a firm cartilaginous
"rind" and soft interior; pileal flesh ordinarily at
least 3-5 mm thick at the center, rarely thin enough
to be called membranous 85

72. Spores white to pale cream-color.....................73
72. Spores pink, dingy salmon-pink, brownish salmon,
yellowish brown, umbrinous, cinnamon brown, purplish
brown, purple, or black 75

73. Stipe tough and elastic to corneous and rigid; pileal context usually pliable and rather tough (marcescent)* .. *Marasmius* (K57, M80, SM109, S135, 155)

73. Stipe soft and fleshy, or brittle and fragile; pileal context easily torn or broken when fresh and moist (not marcescent) 74

   74. Mature pileus parabolic or bell-shaped, or at least deeply convex; pileal margin straight in unexpanded sporocarps, not inrolled . . . .*Mycena* (K778, M93, S134)

   74. Mature pileus plane to shallowly convex; pileal margin inrolled at first . . . . *Collybia* (749, M89, SM105, S135)

75. (72) Spores pink or ochraceous salmon or brownish salmon (mature gills becoming more or less pink from the spores) 76

75. Spores some shade of yellowish brown or cinnamon brown or bright rusty brown, or in the purple-brown series, or black 77

   76. Mature pileus parabolic or bell-shaped, or at least deeply convex; pileal margin straight in unexpanded sporocarps, not inrolled . . . . *Nolanea* (K579; see *Rhodophyllus* M109, SM114, S201)

   76. Mature pileus plane to shallowly convex; pileal margin inrolled in unexpanded sporocarps . . . .*Leptonia* (571, see *Rhodophyllus* M109, SM114, S201)

77. (75) Spores yellow-brown to cinnamon-brown or rusty brown ..78

77. Spores purple-brown or black 81

   78. Pileus viscid 79

   78. Pileus not viscid 80

79. Spores bright rusty brown or orange-brown; unexpanded pilei conical to bell-shaped, with straight margin . . . .*Bolbitius* (K502, M132)

79. Spores cinnamon-brown to umber; unexpanded pilei convex, with inrolled margin . . . .*Naucoria* (K508, M134)

*Marcescent = able to revive when moistened; does not putrify when drying.

80. (78) Pileus conical to parabolic or bell-shaped,
the margin at first straight .... *Galerina* (K49
M132, SM134, S21£

80. Pileus convex to flat, the margin at first
incurved or inrolled .... *Naucoria* (K508, M13

81. (77) Spores purple-brown or fuscous purple .... .82

81. Spores black .... .84

82 Pileus viscid .... *Psilocybe* (K27
M122, SM21£

82. Pileus not viscid .... .83

83. Mature pilei bell-shaped or parabolic or conical, the
margin at first straight .... *Psathyre.*
(K268, M11£

83. Mature pilei convex to plane, the margin at first
strongly in curved or inrolled .... *Psilocybe* (K27
M122, SM21£

84. (81) Gills mottled from the ripening of the spores
in patches; pileal margin not sulcate or plicate-
striate; sporocarps mostly growing on dung .... *Panaeolus* (K22
M117, SM15£

84. Gills not mottled; pileus sulcate or plicate-striate;
sporocarps not growing on dung .... *Psathyrella* (K22
M118) (see also sma
species of *Coprinu*

85. (71) Spores white to pale cream-color (rarely cream-
color with a faint pinkish tinge) .... .86

85. Spores pink, brown, or purple-brown .... .88

86. Gills thick, subdistant, and usually very soft
and waxy-appearing 86A

86. Gills thin, usually close or crowded, rarely
subdistant, and not waxy-appearing .... .87

86A. Gills purple vinaceous red to flesh color,
often thick and rather hard & brittle .... *Laccaria* (M9£
SM103, S135

86A. Gills usually colored otherwise, usually
soft .... *Hygrophorus* (K17
M38, SM69, S229

7. Stipe with a rigid, firm, cartilaginous (brittle)
     "rind", and the interior soft, or sometimes hollow 87A

   87. Stipe of a more or less uniform pulpy or fleshy-
     fibrous texture . . . . *Tricholoma* (K675,
                                            M102, SM48, S150)

7A. Gills adnate or broadly adnexed . . . . *Clitocybe* (K715, M84)

7A. Gills sinuate or notched . . . . *Tricholoma* (K675,
                                            M102, SM48, S150)

   88. (85) Spores pink, dingy salmon, or brownish salmon 89

   88. Spores some shade of brown or purple-brown 90

9. Mature gills becoming definitely pink form the spores . . . . *Entoloma*
                            (K545; see *Rhodophyllus* M109,
                                         SM114, S201)

9. Mature gills not pink from the spores . . . . *Tricholoma* (K675,
                                            M102, SM48, S150)

   90. (88 Spores yellow-brown, umber, cinnamon-brown
     or rusty-brown 91

   90. Spores purple-brown or fuscous purple . . . . *Hypholoma* (K254,
                                             M119)

. Hymenophore separable as a unit from the pileal flesh;
     gills often strongly intervenose at the stipe, often
     quickly staining reddish brown where bruised . . . . *Paxillus* (K284,
                                            M130, SM128, S204)

. Hymenophore not separating as a unit from the pileus
     (though ***individual gills*** may break off readily); gills
     not as in the above in the other particulars 92

   92. Pileus viscid 93

   92. Pileus not viscid 96

. Spores bright rusty brown or orange-brown 94

. Spores cinnamon-brown or umber or dull brown 95

   94. Cortina present, usually abundant and readily seen
     in unexpanded pilei; stipe not deeply radicating . . . . *Cortinarius* (K314,
                                            M145, SM125, S202)

   94. No trace of a cortina, or any other kind of partial
     veil, even in the youngest specimens; stipe deeply
     radicating . . . .*Naucoria* (K508,
                                            M134)

78

95. (93) Gills of mature specimens grayish cinnamon or dull
grayish yellow-brown, almost always with conspicuously
white edges .... *Hebeloma* (K468
M144, SM128)

95. Gills of mature specimens rather bright yellowish brown,
or rust-color, or dark smoky brown .... *Flammula* (K483
M140)

96. (92) Sporocarps lignicolous 97

96. Sporocarps terrestrial 98

97. Spores and mature gills bright orange-brown
or rust-colored .... *Flammula* (K483
M140)

97. Spores and mature gills dull grayish umber .... *Inocybe* (K442
M142, SM131

98. (96) Spores and mature gills bright orange-brown
or deep, rich, rusty-brown; cortina present and
obvious in unexpanded pilei .... *Cortinarius* (K314
M145, SM125, S202

98. Spores and mature gills dull grayish umber, or a
similar dull or grayish brown; a cortina may be
present in unexpanded pilei, but rather more
frequently it is lacking, or very poorly developed ..... *Inocybe* (K442
M142, SM131

V. LITERATURE CITED

Kauffman, C. H. 1965. *The Agaricaceae of Michigan.* Johnson Reprint Corp.

Lange, M. and F. B. Hora. 1967. *A Guide to Mushrooms and Toadstools.* New York: E. P. Dutton & Co., Inc.

McKenny, M. 1962. *Savory Wild Mushroom.* Revised and Enlarged by D. E. Stuntz. Univ. Wash. Press; Seattle, Wash.

Miller, O. K. Jr. 1972. *Mushrooms of North America.* New York: E. P. Dutton & Co., Inc.

Smith, A. H. 1949. *Mushrooms in their Natural Habitat.* Sawyers, Inc. Portland, Ore.

Smith, A. H. 1963. *Mushroom Hunter's Field Guide;* revised and enlarged. Univ. of Mich. Press; Ann Arbor, Mich.

80

INDEX

(* = Illustration)

84

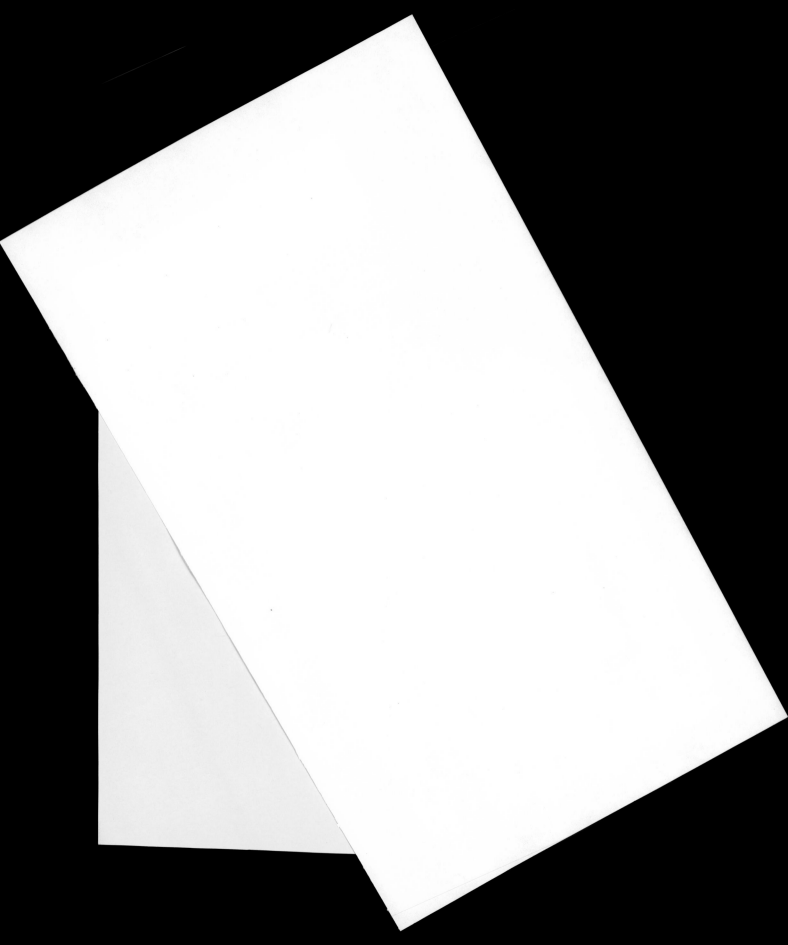